THE CONTEMPORARY CHRISTIAN BOOK

ISBN-13: 978-0-634-05603-1

HAL•LEONARD® CORPORATION

7777 W. BLUEMOUND RD. P.O. BOX 13819 MILWAUKEE, WI 53213

THE CONTEMPORARY CHRISTIAN

CONTENTS

Abba
(Father)

Words and Music by Rebecca St. James, Tedd Tjornhom and Otto Price

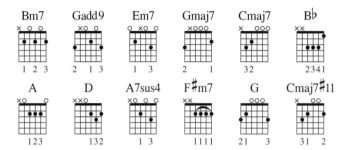

Strum Pattern: 4, 6
Pick Pattern: 2, 4

Verse
Moderately fast

1. I'm feel-ing like the ea - gle that ris - es, flies a-bove the earth and its trou-bles.
2. Run-ning in this race 'til the fin-ish line, the on-ly road for me is the nar-row.

Oh, yes, He knows that there are val-leys be-low, but un-der His wings there's a strong-er pow - er.
Not gon-na stop or e-ven look to the side when I fix my eyes on You, Je - sus.

Oh, Fa - ther, You are my strength. On You I wait up-on.
Oh, Fa - ther, You are my strength, now more than ev - er.

% Chorus

You make the road rise up to meet me. You make the sun-sine warm up-on my face.

To Coda 1 ⊕ |1.
To Coda 2 ⊕

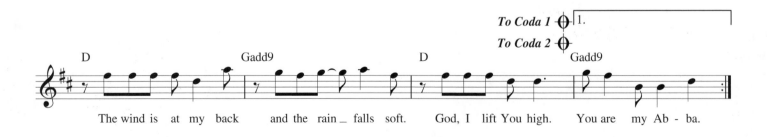

The wind is at my back and the rain falls soft. God, I lift You high. You are my Ab - ba.

You are my Ab - ba.

You are my Ab - ba. When you run too far, can't
(And the road is long.

walk an-oth - er mile, hope in Him a - gain. Then
He is wait - ing. He'll re - new you.)

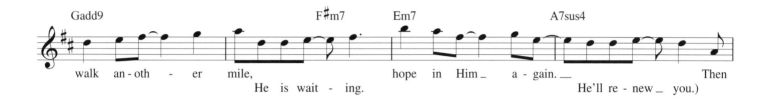

you will rise. Gath-er up your wings and fly.

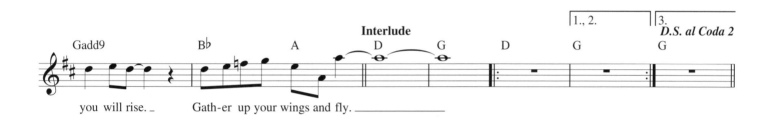

You are my Ab - ba. *Spoken:* Do you not know?

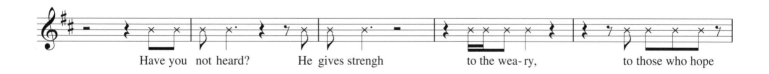

Have you not heard? He gives strengh to the wea-ry, to those who hope

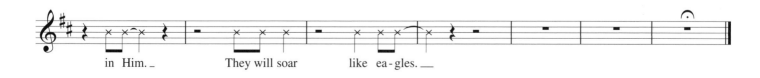

in Him. They will soar like ea-gles.

Above All

Words and Music by Paul Baloche and Lenny LeBlanc

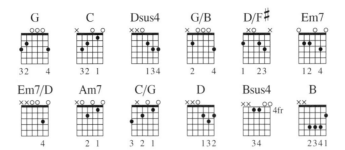

Strum Pattern: 6
Pick Pattern: 4

Verse

Moderately slow

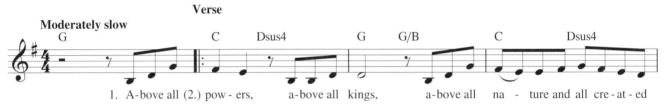

1. A-bove all (2.) pow - ers, a-bove all kings, a-bove all na - ture and all cre-at-ed

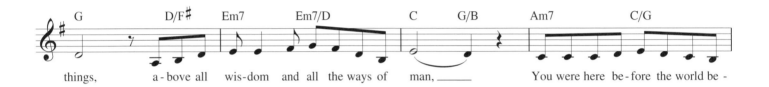

things, a - bove all wis-dom and all the ways of man, _____ You were here be-fore the world be -

gan. A-bove all king - doms, a-bove all thrones, a-bove all won - ders the world has ev - er

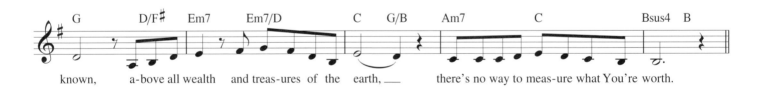

known, a-bove all wealth and treas-ures of the earth, _____ there's no way to meas-ure what You're worth.

% Chorus

Cru - ci-fied, _ laid be-hind _ the stone. You lived to die, _ re - ject-ed and a-lone. Like a rose _

To Coda ⊕

_____ tram-pled on _ the ground, You took _ the fall, _ and thought of me _

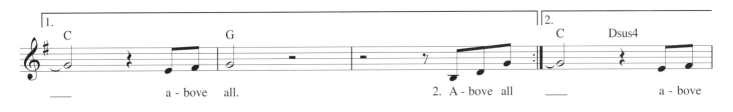

a - bove all. 2. *A - bove all* ___ *a - bove*

D.S. al Coda **Coda** **Outro**

all. ___ *a - bove all. Like a rose tram-pled on* ___ *the*

ground, *You took* ___ *the fall,* ___ *and thought of me* ___ *a - bove all.*

Awesome God

Words and Music by Rich Mullins

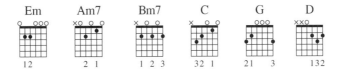

Strum Pattern: 1, 2
Pick Pattern: 4, 5

Verse

Moderately

1. *When He rolls up His sleeve,* ___ *He ain't just "put - tin' on the Ritz." Our*
   sky ___ *was star - less in the void* ___ *of the night, our*

God is an awe - some God! *There is thun - der in His foot-steps and light - nin' in His fist. Our*
God is an awe - some God! *He spoke in - to the dark - ness and cre - at - ed the light. Our*

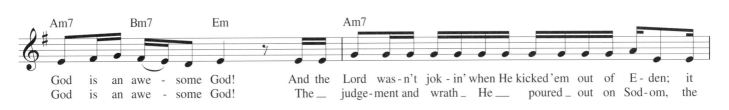

God is an awe - some God! *And the Lord was - n't jok - in' when He kicked 'em out of E - den; it*
God is an awe - some God! *The* ___ *judge-ment and wrath* ___ *He* ___ *poured* ___ *out on Sod - om, the*

was-n't for no rea-son that He shed His _ blood. His re - turn is ver - y close and so you bet-ter be be-liev-in' that our
mer-cy and grace _ He gave us at the _ cross. I hope that we have _ not too quick - ly for-got-ten that our

Chorus

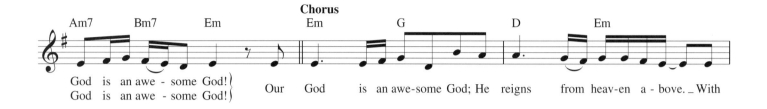

God is an awe - some God!{
God is an awe - some God!{ Our God is an awe-some God; He reigns from heav-en a - bove. _ With

wis - dom, pow'r and love, our God is an awe - some _ God! Our God is an awe-some God; He

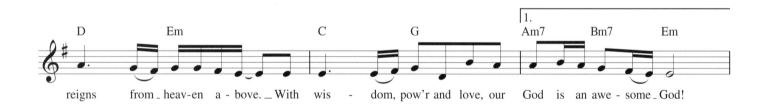

reigns from _ heav-en a - bove. _ With wis - dom, pow'r and love, our God is an awe - some _ God!

*Use Pattern 10

2. And when the God is an awe - some _ God! Our

Outro-Chorus

God is an awe-some God; He reigns from _ heav-en a - bove. _ With wis - dom, pow'r and love, our

God is an awe - some _ God! Our God is an awe-some God! Our God is an awe - some _ God!

Beautiful

**Words and Music by Mark Stuart, Will McGinniss,
Bob Herdman, Tyler Burkum and Ben Cissell**

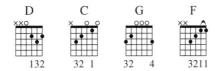

Strum Pattern: 2, 5
Pick Pattern: 1

Intro
Moderately

* Strum chords in indicated rhythm.

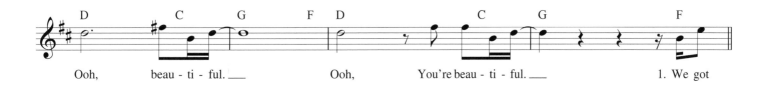

Ooh,   beau - ti - ful. ___   Ooh,   You're beau - ti - ful. ___   1. We got

mu - sic   to soothe your ___ soul.   We're gon-na get down with a lit-tle bit of rock and roll. _
2. *See additional lyrics*

___   We got   rhy - thm   to move your ___ feet.   We're gon-na

% Chorus

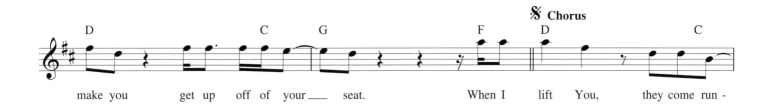

make you   get up   off of your ___ seat.   When I   lift   You,   they come run -

-ning. When I sing Your song, the world's turn - ing to You. Just the sound

To Coda ⊕

____ of Your name is a beau - ti - ful thing. ___ And I love ___ You, I love ___ You, I love

1. | 2.

* Use Pattern 10

___ You. 2. Your ___ You. Just the sound ___ of Your name is a beau -

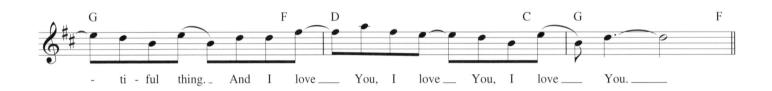

- ti - ful thing. ___ And I love ___ You, I love ___ You, I love ___ You. ___

Interlude

Do, do, do, do, do, do, do, do, do, do, do, do, do, do, do, do, do, do,

Bridge

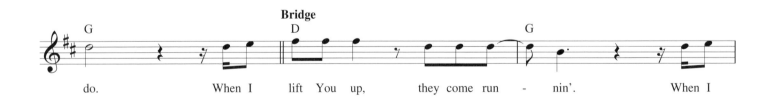

do. When I lift You up, they come run - nin'. When I

sing Your song, the world's turn - ing. Just the sound ___ of Your name is a beau -

- ti - ful thing. And I love ___ You, I love ___ You, I love ___ You. When I

Coda

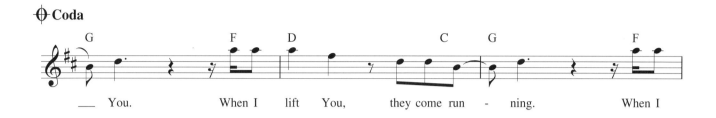

___ You. When I lift You, they come run - ning. When I

sing Your song, the world's turn - ing to You. Just the sound ___ of Your name is a beau-

- ti - ful thing. ___ And I love ___ You, I love ___ You, I love ___ You. I say,

Outro

do, do, do, do, do, do, do, do, do, do, do, do, do, do, do, do, do, do, do.

Repeat and fade

Do, do, do, do, do, do, do, do, do, do, do, do, do, do, do, do, do, do, do.

Additional Lyrics

2. Your name is beautiful
   It drips off of my lips like drops of gold.
   It makes me want to dance.
   You're my treasure, my deliverance.

Always Have, Always Will

Words and Music by Grant Cunningham, Nick Gonzales and Toby McKeehan

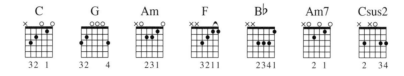

Strum Pattern: 6
Pick Pattern: 4

Verse
Moderately

1. Part of me __ is the pro - di - gal, part of me __ is the oth - er broth - er.
2. I was born __ with a way - ward heart; still I live __ with the rest - less spir - it.

But I ____ think the heart of me is real - ly some - where be - tween __ them.
My soul __ is so well worn you'd think I'd have _____ ar - rived by now.

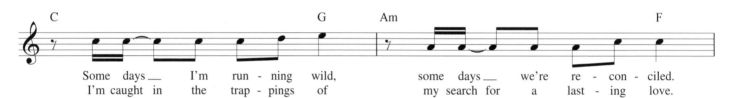

Some days __ I'm run - ning wild, some days __ we're re - con - ciled.
I'm caught in the trap - pings of my search for a last - ing love.

But I won - der all ___ the while __ why You put __ up with me, ___ when
I've made mis - takes __ e - nough to last me __ a life - time.

I wres - tle most ___ days __ to find ___ ways __ to
Still slip, __ I still __ fall. __ But I'll ___ al - ways

𝄋 Chorus

do as __ I please. I ___ { al - ways _ have. _ I al - ways _ will. ____ You saved _
run back _ to you. I ___ {

___ me _ once. You save __ me _ still. __ {1. A} long - ing __ heart Your love _
{2., 3. My}

Because of Your Love

Words and Music by Paul Baloche and Brenton Brown

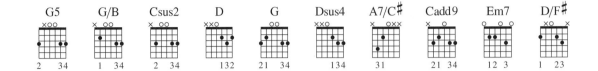

Between You and Me

Words and Music by Toby McKeehan and Mark Heimermann

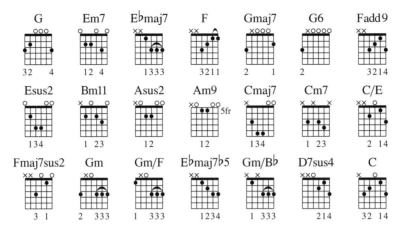

Strum Pattern: 2, 6
Pick Pattern: 4

Cry Out to Jesus

Words by Mac Powell
Music by Mac Powell, David Carr, Tai Anderson, Brad Avery and Mark Lee

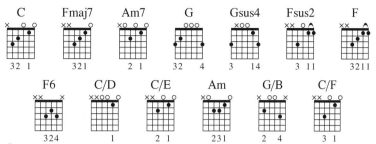

Strum Pattern: 7, 8
Pick Pattern: 7, 8

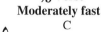 **Verse**
Moderately fast

1. To ev - er - y - one who's lost some - one they love   long be - fore __ it was their __
2. *See additional lyrics*

time, __   you feel like the days __ you had __ were not e - nough __ when you said __

__ good- bye.   And to all of the peo - ple with bur - dens and

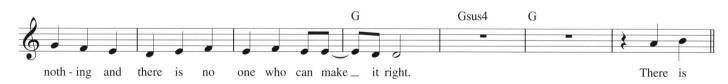

pains   keep - ing you __ back from your __ life, __   you be - lieve that there's __

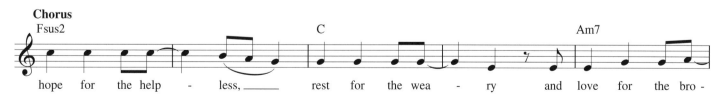

noth - ing and there is no one who can make __ it right.   There is

Chorus

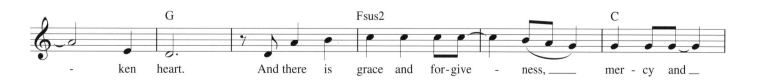

hope for the help - less, __ rest for the wea - ry and love for the bro -

- ken heart. And there is grace and for - give - ness, __ mer - cy and __

To Coda ⊕

Am7 / G / F Fmaj7

heal - ing; He'll meet you wher - ev - er you_ are. Cry out_ to Je - sus. ____

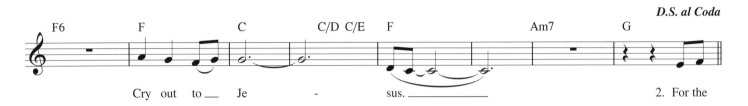

D.S. al Coda

F6 / F / C / C/D C/E F / Am7 / G

Cry out to_ Je - sus. _____ 2. For the

⊕ Coda

Fsus2 **Bridge** Am

Cry out __ to Je - sus. _____ When you're _ lone-ly, _

G/B C F

and it ___ feels like the whole _ world is fall - ing on you,

Am Gsus4 F C/F F

you just _ reach out, _ you just _ cry out to Je - sus, _____

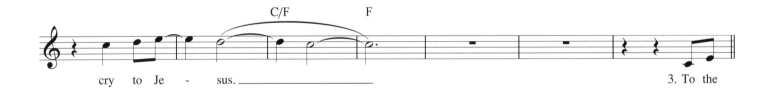

C/F F

cry to Je - sus. _____ 3. To the

Verse
C Fmaj7

wid - ow who suf - fers from be - ing a - lone, wip - ing the tears __ from her _

Am7

eyes, and for the chil - dren a - round __ the world _ with-out a home, say a prayer _

Outro-Chorus

_____ to - night. _____ There is _____ hope for the help - less, _____

rest for the wea - ry and love for the bro - ken heart. And there is

grace and for-give - ness, _____ mer - cy and _ heal - ing; He'll meet you wher - ev - er you _

are. There is _____ Cry out _ to Je - sus. _____ Cry out _ to

Je - sus. _____

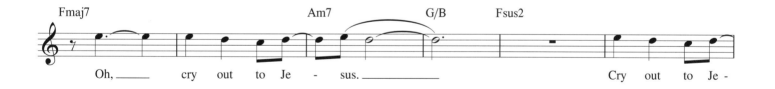

Oh, _____ cry out to Je - sus. _____ Cry out to Je -

- sus. _____

Additional Lyrics

2. For the marriage that's struggling just to hang on,
   They've lost all of their faith in love,
   And they've done all they can to make it right again,
   Still it's not enough.
   For the ones who can't break the addictions and chains,
   You try to give up but you come back again,
   Just remember that you're not alone in your shame
   And your suffering.

Blessed Be Your Name

Words and Music by Matt Redman and Beth Redman

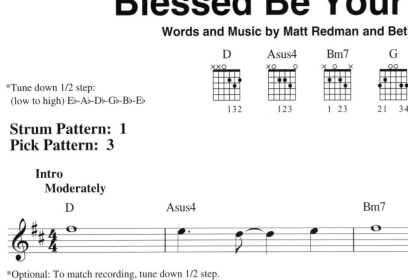

*Tune down 1/2 step:
(low to high) Eb-Ab-Db-Gb-Bb-Eb

Strum Pattern: 1
Pick Pattern: 3

Intro
Moderately

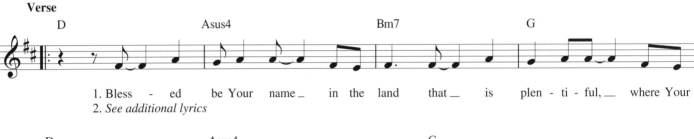

*Optional: To match recording, tune down 1/2 step.

Verse

1. Bless - ed be Your name _ in the land that _ is plen - ti - ful, _ where Your
2. *See additional lyrics*

streams of __ a - bun - dance flow, _ bless - ed be Your name.

Bless - ed be Your name _ when I'm found in __ the des - ert place, _ though I

walk through _ the wil - der - ness, _ bless - ed be Your name.

Pre-Chorus

Ev - 'ry bless - ing You pour out I'll turn back to praise.

When the dark - ness clos - es in, Lord, _ still I will say: Bless-ed be the

Additional Lyrics

2. Blessed be Your name when the sun's shining down on me,
   When the world's all as it should be, blessed be Your name.
   Blessed be Your name on the road marked with suffering.
   Though there's pain in the offering, blessed be Your name.

Can't Live a Day

Words and Music by Ty Lacy, Connie Harrington and Joe Beck

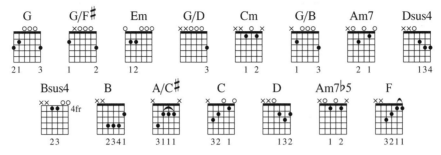

Strum Pattern: 4
Pick Pattern: 4

Verse
Moderately

1. I could live life a-lone ___ and nev-er fill ___ the long-
2. I could trav-el the world, ___ see all the won-ders beau-

-ings of ___ my heart, ___ the heal-ing warmth ___ of some - one's arms. And I
-ti-ful ___ and new. ___ They'd on - ly make ___ me think ___ of You. And I

___ could live with-out ___ dreams, ___ and nev-er know ___ the thrill ___
___ could have all life ___ of-fered, rich - es that ___ were far

___ of what ___ could be ___ with ev-'ry star ___ so far ___ and out ___ of
___ be - yond ___ com-pare, ___ to grant my ev - 'ry wish ___ with-out ___ a

reach. I could live with-out ___ man - y things _____ and I
care. Oh, I could do ___ an - y-thing. oh, yes. But if

% Chorus

___ could car - ry on. ___ But I \} I could-n't face ___ my life ___ to-mor - row with-out Your hope
You weren't in ___ it all, ___ I \}

*Sung one octave higher (8va)

___ in my ___ heart. I know ___ I can't live a day with - out ___ You. ___

Dare You to Move

Words and Music by Jonathan Foreman

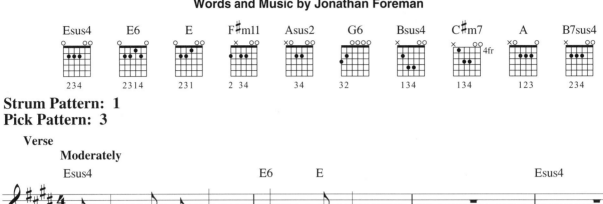

Strum Pattern: 1
Pick Pattern: 3

Verse
Moderately

1. Wel-come to the plan - et. ___

Wel - come to ex - ist - ence. ___

Ev - 'ry-one's ___ here. ___ Ev - 'ry-one's ___ here. ___

Ev - 'ry-bod-y's watch - ing ___ you ___ now. ___

Ev - 'ry-bod-y waits ___ for you ___ now. ___

What hap - pens next? ___ What hap - pens next? ___ I

%. Chorus

dare you to move. ___ I dare you to move. ___ I

dare you to lift ___ your - self up ___ off the floor. ___ I

Dive

Words and Music by Steven Curtis Chapman

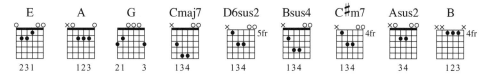

*Tune down 1/2 step:
(low to high) E♭-A♭-D♭-G♭-B♭-E♭

Strum Pattern: 2
Pick Pattern: 4

*Optional: To match recording, tune down 1/2 step.

Verse

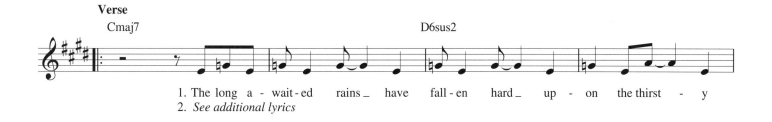

1. The long a-wait-ed rains __ have fall-en hard __ up-on the thirst __ y
2. *See additional lyrics*

ground. They've carved their way to where __ the wild and rush - ing

riv - er can ____ be found. And like the rain, I have been

car - ried here ___ to where the riv - er flows. Yeah. ___

___ My heart is rac - ing ___ and my

knees are weak ___ as I walk to ___ the edge. I know there

is no turn - ing back a once my feet have left ___ the

ledge. And in the rush, I hear a voice that's tell - ing

me it's time ___ to take the leap ___ of faith. ___ So here ___ I go. ___

𝄋 Chorus

___ I'm div - ing in. ___ I'm go - ing deep, ___ in o - ver my

head. I wan - na be ___ caught in the rush, ___ lost in the flow. ___

In o-ver my head I wan-na go. ___ The riv-er's deep, ___

___ the riv-er's wide, ___ the riv-er's wa - ter is a - live. ___

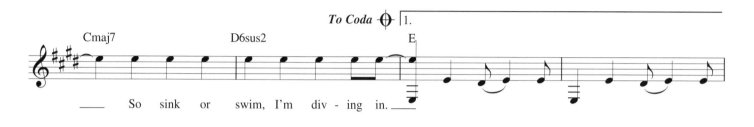

To Coda ⊕ |1.

___ So sink or swim, I'm div-ing in. ___

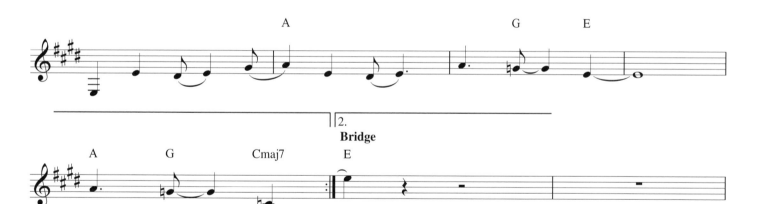

|2.

Bridge

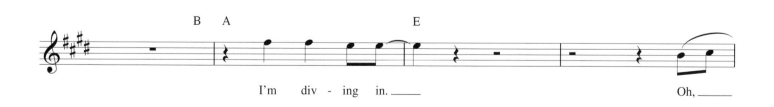

I'm div - ing in. ___ Oh, ___

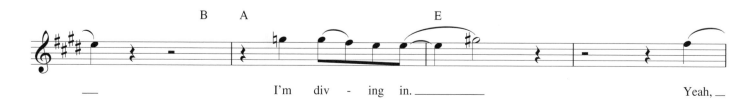

___ I'm div - ing in. ___ Yeah, ___

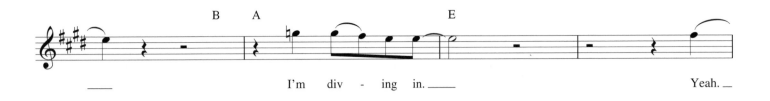

I'm div - ing in. ____ Yeah. ____

Interlude

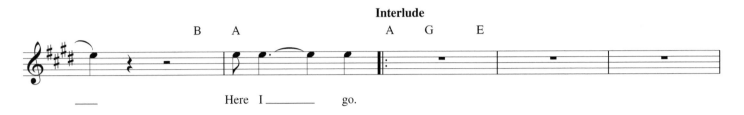

Here I ____ go.

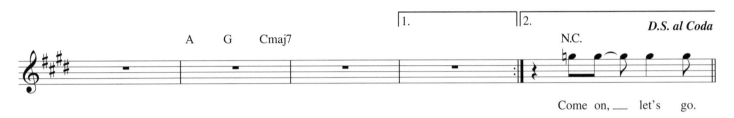

Come on, ____ let's go.

So sink or swim, ____ I'm div - ing in. ____ So sink or

Outro

swim, I'm div - ing in. ____ Whoa. ____

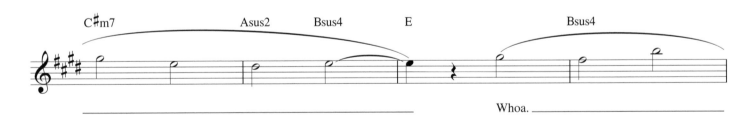

Whoa. ____

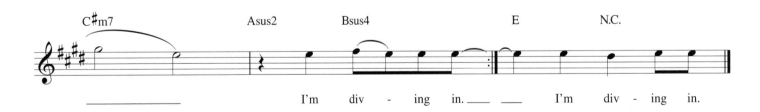

I'm div - ing in. ____ ____ I'm div - ing in.

Additional Lyrics

2. There is a supernatural power in this mighty river's flow.
It can bring the dead to life and it can fill an empty soul,
And give our heart the only thing worth living and worth dying for, yeah.
But we will never know the awesome power of the grace of God
Until we let ourselves get swept away into this holy flood.
So if you take my hand, we'll close our eyes and count to three,
And take the leap of faith. Come on let's go.

Favorite Song of All

Words and Music by Dan Dean

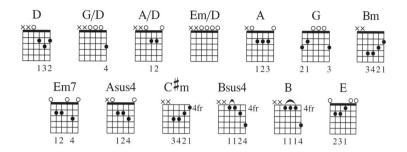

Strum Pattern: 3, 4
Pick Pattern: 4, 5

Verse
Moderately

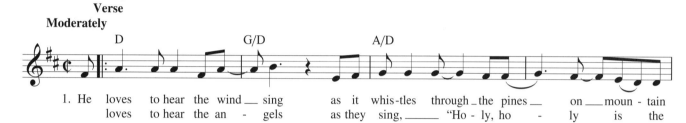

1. He loves to hear the wind __ sing as it whis-tles through __ the pines __ on __ moun - tain
loves to hear the an - gels as they sing, _____ "Ho - ly, ho - ly is the

peaks. _____ And He loves to hear the rain - drops as they
Lamb." _____ Heav - en's choirs in har - mo-ny

splash to the ground in a mag-ic mel - o - dy. _____ He
lift up prais - es to the great __ "I _____ Am." _____ But He

smiles in __ sweet ap - prov - al as the waves crash __ to the rocks __ in har - mo - ny. __
lifts His hands __ for si - lence when the weak - est saved by grace be - gins to sing __

Cre - a - tion joins __ in _____ u - ni - ty __ to
and a mil-lion an - gels lis - ten __ as a

sing to Him __ ma - jes - tic sym - pho - nies. _____ But
new-born soul sings,"I have been _____ re - deemed." __ 'Cause } His fav - 'rite song of

Chorus

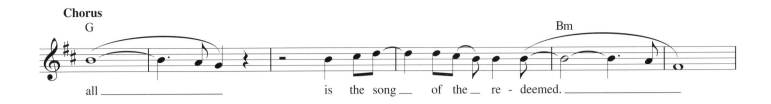

all _____ is the song ___ of the ___ re - deemed. _____

When lost sin-ners now ___ made clean ___ lift their voic - es loud ___ and

strong; _____ when those pur-chased by ___ His blood _____ lift to Him ___

___ a song ___ of love; _____ there's noth-ing more ___ He'd rath-er hear, ___

___ nor so pleas - ing to ___ His ear, _____ as His fav - 'rite song _____

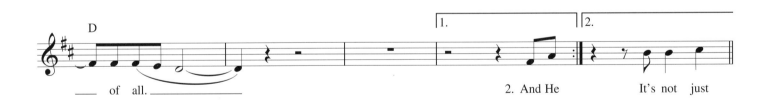

1.

___ of all. _____ 2. And He

2.

It's not just

Bridge

mel - o - dies ___ and har - mo - nies ___ that catch - es His ___ at - ten - tion. It's not just

clev - er lines ___ and phras - es that caus - es ___ Him to stop ___ and lis - ten. But when

an - y heart set free, _____ washed and bought _ by Cal - va - ry, ____ be - gins _ to sing, _

Chorus

that's his fav - 'rite _ song of all: _____ is the song _

_ of the _ re - deemed. _____ When lost sin - ners now _ made clean _

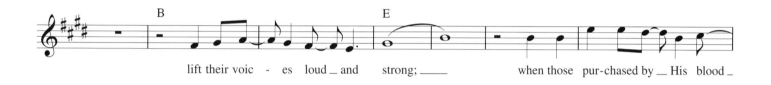

lift their voic - es loud _ and strong; ____ when those pur-chased by _ His blood _

_____ lift to Him _ a song _ of love; _____ there's noth-ing more _

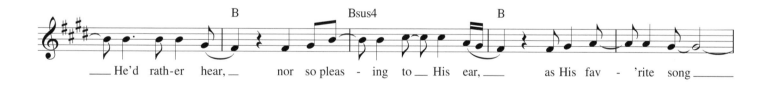

_ He'd rath-er hear, _ nor so pleas - ing to _ His ear, ___ as His fav - 'rite song ____

Outro

_ of all. _____ Ho - ly, ho - ly, ho - ly is _ the Lamb. _

_____ Hal - le - lu - jah. Hal - le - lu - jah. ____

Down on My Knees

Words and Music by Wayne Kirkpatrick

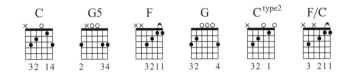

C   G5   F   G   C^{type2}   F/C

*Capo II

Strum Pattern: 3, 4
Pick Pattern: 4, 5

Verse

Rhythmically

1. I've got a wit-ness not __ too sta - ble.   It would-n't get me ver - y far. __
   bit - ter winds __ grow cold - er,   they are danc-ing with __ my pride. __

*Optional: To match recording, place capo at 2nd fret.

__ I've got __ one hand on the ta - ble and one in the cook - ie jar. __
__ I've got a chip __ on my shoul - der big-ger than a moun-tain - side. __

I've got sins that need __ e - vic - tion   from a tem - ple that's __ a wreck.
And these claws of hu - man na - ture   hold me tight with - in ____ their clasp.

I've got a chain of con - tra - dic - tion   hang-ing a - round __ my neck. __ }
I'm not wor - thy of for-give - ness,   but I just have to ask. __ }

So, I go down, __ I go down, __ down, I go down __ on my knees. __

1.

__ 2. I feel the __

2.   **𝄋 Chorus**

Feed my hun-

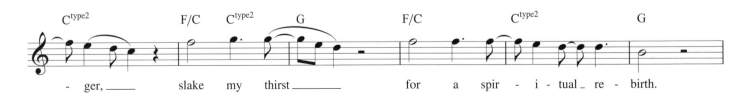

- ger, ____ slake my thirst ____ for a spir - i - tual __ re - birth.

Dying to Reach You

Words and Music by Michael Puryear and Geoffrey Thurman

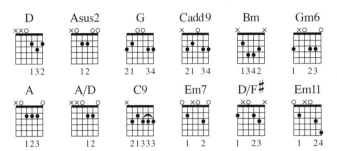

*Capo I

Strum Pattern: 1
Pick Pattern: 1

Intro   Verse
Moderately

1. He looked through tem-ples of time __ to see you right where you stand. __
2. *See additional lyrics*

*Optional: To match recording, place capo at 1st fret.

He emp-tied all of Him-self __ so He could reach out His hand _____

to give hope _ and mean - ing ____ to the wast-ed __ a - way. ____

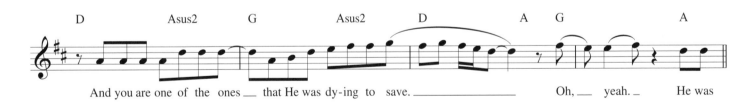

And you are one of the ones __ that He was dy-ing to save. _____ Oh, __ yeah. _ He was

Chorus

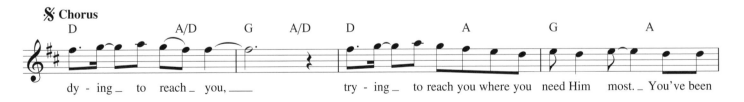

dy - ing _ to reach _ you, ___ try - ing _ to reach you where you need Him most. _ You've been

liv - ing _ in search _ of _____ the whole truth _ and real _ love your whole life through. _ You can

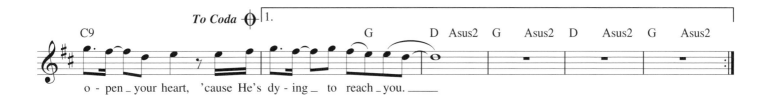

o - pen _ your heart, 'cause He's dy - ing _ to reach _ you. _____

dy - ing _ to reach you. _   Oh, He has wait - ed time _ and time be - fore. _____

You must _ be still ____ and know _ that He is Lord. _____

3. He was dy - ing to reach you, _____   try - ing to reach you where you need Him the most. _

Tell me, what are you look - ing for? Won't you   o - pen your heart? ____ He's dy - ing _ to reach you,

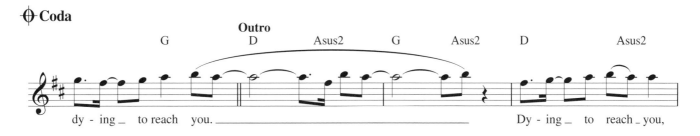

dy - ing _ to reach you. _____   Dy - ing _ to reach _ you,

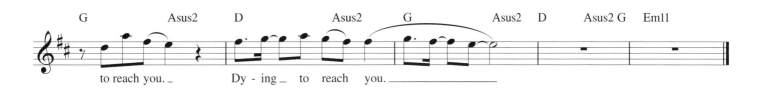

to reach you. _   Dy - ing _ to reach you. _____

Additional Lyrics

2. He's standing there at the door,
   You can hear Him call your name.
   He simply waits to forgive
   All the guilt and the shame.
   He gave up His own life
   And He still bears the scars.
   He only wants to receive you,
   So come as you are.

El Shaddai

Words and Music by Michael Card and John Thompson

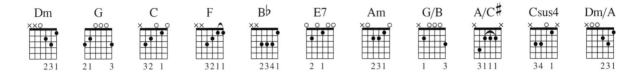

Dm   G   C   F   Bb   E7   Am   G/B   A/C#   Csus4   Dm/A

Strum Pattern: 2, 3
Pick Pattern: 2, 4

% Chorus

Moderately

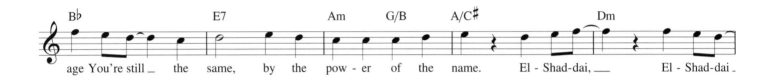

El - Shad-dai, ___ El - Shad-dai, ___ El - El - yon - na A - do - nai, age to

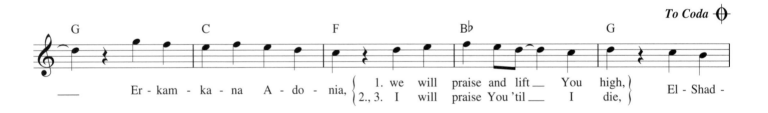

age You're still ___ the same, by the pow - er of the name. El - Shad-dai, ___ El - Shad-dai _

To Coda

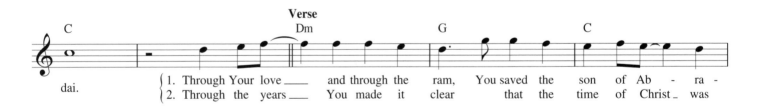

___ Er - kam - ka - na A - do - nia, { 1. we will praise and lift ___ You high, } El - Shad-
{ 2., 3. I will praise You 'til ___ I die, }

Verse

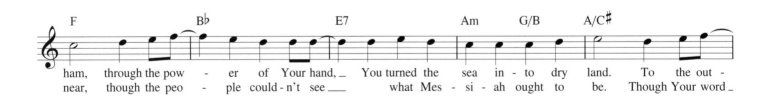

dai. { 1. Through Your love ___ and through the ram, You saved the son of Ab - ra -
{ 2. Through the years ___ You made it clear that the time of Christ ___ was

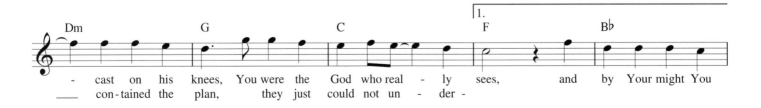

ham, through the pow - er of Your hand, ___ You turned the sea in - to dry land. To the out -
near, though the peo - ple could - n't see ___ what Mes - si - ah ought to be. Though Your word ___

1.

Dm   G   C   F   Bb

- cast on his knees, You were the God who real - ly sees, and by Your might You
___ con - tained the plan, they just could not un - der -

set Your chil - dren free. El - Shad-dai, _ stand, Your most awe - some work was

done in the frail - ty of Your Son. El - Shad-dai, _ dai.

The Glory (Of the Blood)

Words and Music by Regie Hamm and Jim Cooper

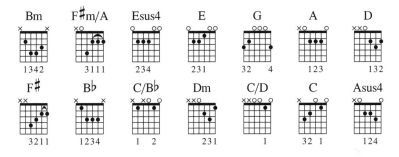

Strum Pattern: 3, 4
Pick Pattern: 4, 5

1. In the sol - i - tar - y mo - ment of _ His birth on this bar - ren dust - y land, _

_ all of heav - en kissed the face of the earth. With a mir - a - cle _ of love,

God be - came _ a man. 2. But He was sent a - way _ to draw His fi - nal breath when He was

3. See additional lyrics

Bm   F#m/A   Esus4   E   Bm   F#m/A

on - ly thir - ty - three. _____ And in the shame of dy - ing a

Esus4   E   G   A

crim - i - nal's ____ death, He cleansed an an - gry world. And in His suf - fer-ing ___ I see ___ the

Chorus
D   G   A   G   F#   Bm

glo - ry of ____ the blood, _____ the beau - ty of ___ the bod - y that was bro -

G   D   A   D   G   D   G

- ken for our for-give - ness. The glo - ry of ____ His per - fect love ___ is the

Bm   A   G   A |1.   Bm   Esus4   E

heart of the sto - ry, the glo - ry ___ of _____ the blood. ___   3. I have

|2.   **Bridge**
D   Bb   C/Bb   Bb   C/Bb

___   And when I close my eyes _ I can see Him hang - ing __ there. _

Dm   C/D   Dm   C/D

Oh, the pre - cious wound - ed Lamb _____ of God! _____

Bb   C/Bb   Bb   C

And all the maj - es - ty ___ in this world can-not ___ com - pare ___ to the glo -

Chorus
D   A   G   F#   Bm

- ry. _____   The beau - ty of ___ the bod - y that was

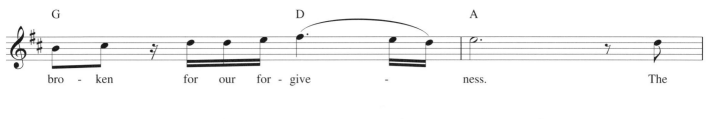

broken for our for-give - ness. The

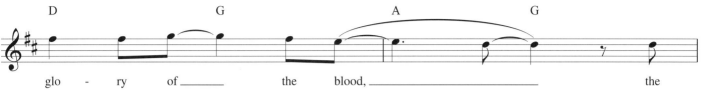

glo - ry of _____ the blood, _____ the

beau - ty of ____ the bod - y that was bro - ken for our for-give - ness. The

glo - ry of ____ His per - fect love ____ is the heart of the sto - ry, the glo -

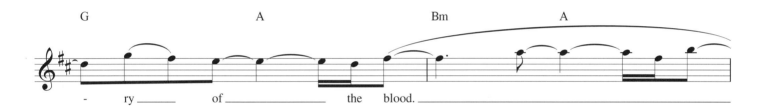

- ry _____ of _____ the blood. _____

Outro

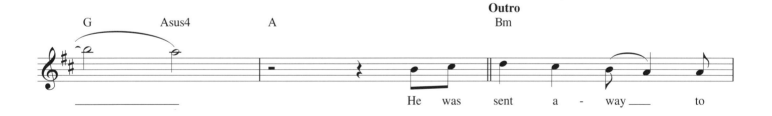

_____ He was sent a - way ____ to

draw His fi - nal breath when He was on - ly thir - ty - three. _____

Additional Lyrics

3. I have tried to find salvation on my own
   In a search for something real.
   There's a guilty heart inside this flesh and bone.
   I fall upon His grace and I begin to feel...

Friends

Words and Music by Michael W. Smith and Deborah D. Smith

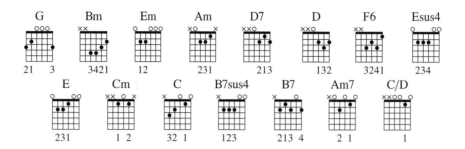

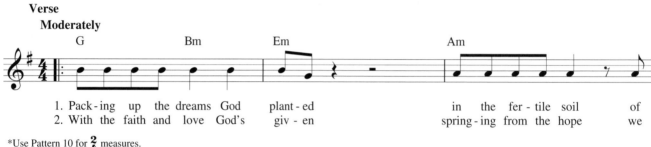

[*]**Strum Pattern: 3, 4**
[*]**Pick Pattern: 3, 4**

Verse
Moderately

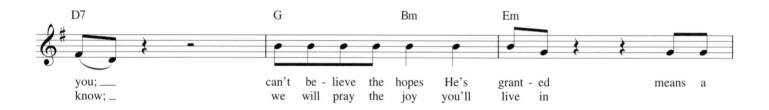

1. Pack - ing up the dreams God plant - ed in the fer - tile soil of
2. With the faith and love God's giv - en spring - ing from the hope we

*Use Pattern 10 for $\frac{2}{4}$ measures.

you; ___ can't be - lieve the hopes He's grant - ed means a
know; _ we will pray the joy you'll live in

Pre-Chorus

chap - ter in your life is through. _ } But we'll keep you close as al - ways; it won't
is the strength that now you show. __ }

e - ven seem you've gone, 'cause our hearts in big and small ways will

keep the love that keeps us strong. And

Chorus

friends are friends for - ev - er if the Lord's the Lord of them. And a friend will not say, "Nev - er" 'cause the

wel - come will not end. Though it's hard to let you go in the

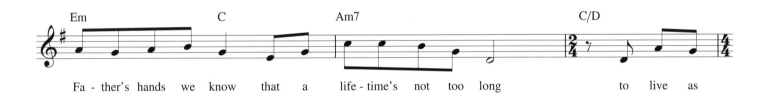

Fa - ther's hands we know that a life - time's not too long to live as

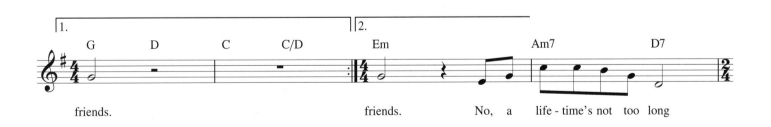

friends. friends. No, a life - time's not too long

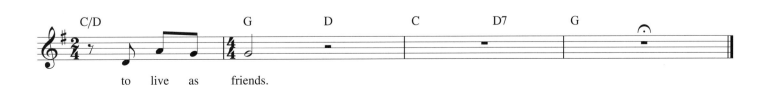

to live as friends.

The Great Adventure

Words and Music by Steven Curtis Chapman and Geoff Moore

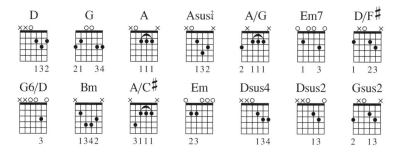

Strum Pattern: 4, 6
Pick Pattern: 4, 5

Verse
Moderately fast Rock

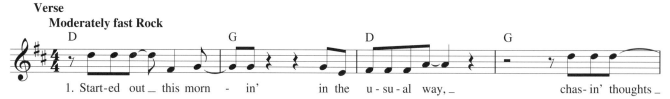

1. Start-ed out this morn - in' in the u-su-al way, chas-in' thoughts

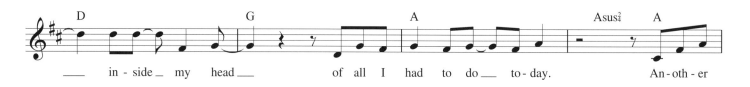

in-side my head of all I had to do to-day. An-oth-er

time a-round the cir - cle, try to make it bet-ter than the last.

Verse

2. I o-pened up the Bi - ble and I read a-bout me.

Said I'd been a pris-'ner and God's grace had set me free. And some-

where be-tween the pag - es, it hit me like a light-ning bolt. I saw a

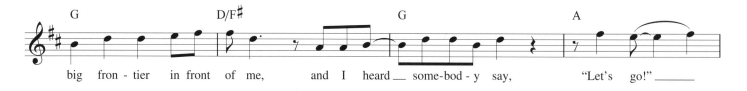

big fron-tier in front of me, and I heard some-bod-y say, "Let's go!"

The Great Divide

Words and Music by Matt Huesmann and Grant Cunningham

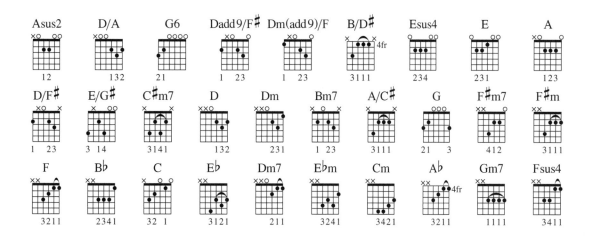

Strum Pattern: 3, 4
Pick Pattern: 4, 5

Verse

Moderately

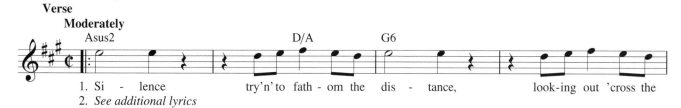

1. Si - lence try'n' to fath - om the dis - tance, look-ing out 'cross the
2. *See additional lyrics*

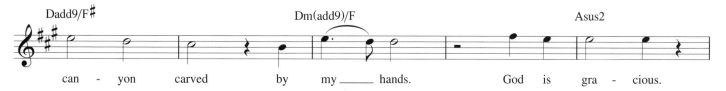

can - yon carved by my ____ hands. God is gra - cious.

Sin would still sep - a - rate us were it not for the bridge His grace has

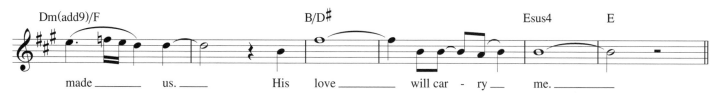

made ____ us. ____ His love ____ will car - ry ____ me. ____

Chorus

There's a bridge ___ to cross ___ the great ___ di - vide, _____ a

way was made ___ to reach ___ the oth - er side. ___ The

mer - cy of ___ the Fa - ther cost His son His life. His love is ___ deep, ___

___ His love is ___ wide. ___ There's a cross to bridge the great ___

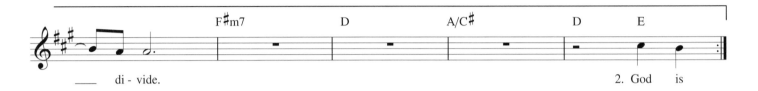

___ di - vide. 2. God is

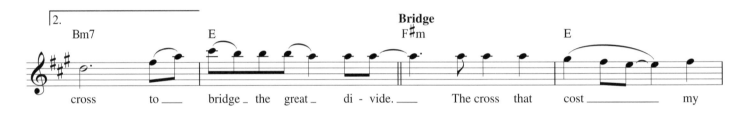

cross to ___ bridge _ the great _ di - vide. ___ The cross that cost ___ my

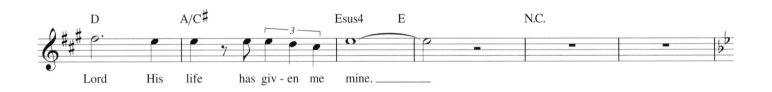

Lord His life has giv - en me mine. ___

There's a bridge _ to cross ___ the great _ di - vide. ___

There's a cross _ to bridge ___ the great _ di - vide. ___

Chorus

There's a bridge _ to cross ___ the great _ di - vide. ___ A

way was made ___ to reach ___ the oth - er side. _____ The

mer - cy of ___ the Fa - ther cost His son His ___ life. His

love is ___ deep, ___ His love is ___ wide. ___ There's a

cross to bridge the great _____ di - vide. _____

Outro-Chorus

There's a cross ___ to bridge ___ the great ___ di - vide, ___ a cross ___ to bridge ___
(There's a ___ cross _____

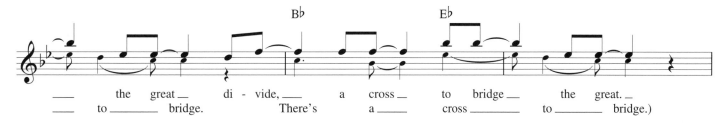

___ the great ___ di - vide, ___ a cross ___ to bridge ___ the great. ___
___ to ___ bridge. There's a ___ cross _____ to ___ bridge.)

There's a cross ___ to bridge ___ the great ___ di - vide. _____

Additional Lyrics

2. God is faithful;
On my own I'm unable.
He found me hopeless, alone
And sent a Savior.
He's provided
A path and promise to guide us
Safely past all the sin
That would divide us.
His love delivers me.

Great Is the Lord

Words and Music by Michael W. Smith and Deborah D. Smith

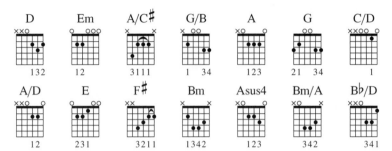

Strum Pattern: 8
Pick Pattern: 8

Verse
Moderately

1., 2. Great is the Lord, He is ho-ly and just. By His pow-er, we trust in His love.

Great is the Lord, He is faith-ful and true. By His mer-cy He proves He is love.

% Chorus

1., 2. Great is the Lord, } and wor-thy of glo-ry.
3. Great are You, Lord, }
Great is the Lord, } and wor-thy of praise.
Great are You, Lord, }

Great is the Lord. Now lift up your voice. Now lift up your voice. Great _____ is the
Great are You, Lord, I lift up my voice. I lift up my voice. Great _____ are You,

To Coda ⊕   **1.**   **2. D.S. al Coda**

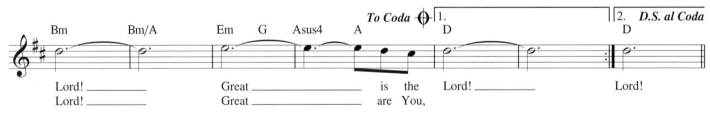

Lord! _____ Great _____ is the Lord! _____ Lord!
Lord! _____ Great _____ are You,

⊕ Coda

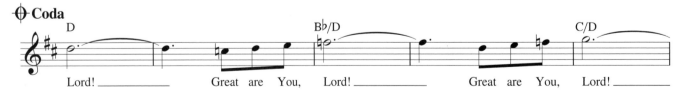

Lord! _____ Great are You, Lord! _____ Great are You, Lord!

____ Great are You, Lord! _____

He Reigns

Words and Music By Peter Furler and Steve Taylor

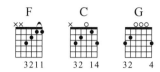

Strum Pattern: 6
Pick Pattern: 5

Verse
Moderately

1. It's the song of the __ re - deemed __ ris - ing from the Af - ri - can __ plain.
rise a - bove _ the four winds caught up in __ the heav - en - ly sound. _

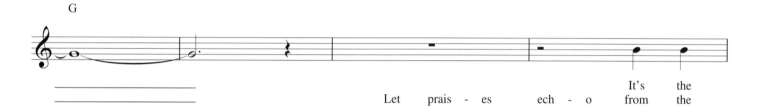

Let prais - es ech - o from the It's the

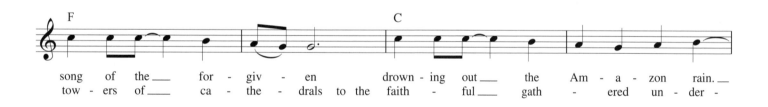

song of the __ for - giv - en drown - ing out __ the Am - a - zon rain. _
tow - ers of __ ca - the - drals to the faith - ful __ gath - ered un - der -

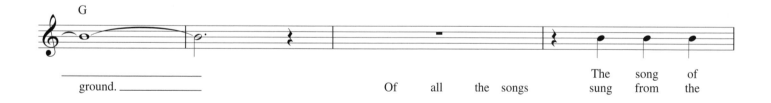

ground. _____ Of all the songs sung from the
The song of

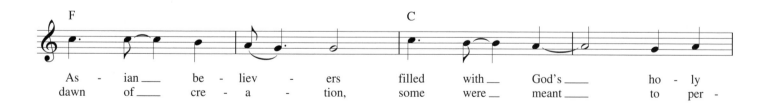

As - ian __ be - liev - ers filled with __ God's __ ho - ly
dawn of __ cre - a - tion, some were __ meant __ to per -

fire. _____ It's ev - 'ry tribe, ev - 'ry
sist. _____ Of all the bells rung from a

tongue, ev - ’ry na - tion, a love song __ born __ of a grate - ful
thou - sand __ stee - ples, none rings __ tru - er than this. __

choir. _____ }
_____

℞ **Chorus**

glo - ry, glo - ry, hal - le - lu - jah, He reigns, _____

__ He reigns. __ { 1., 2. It’s all God’s chil - dren sing - ing } glo - ry, glo -
3. All God’s chil - dren sing out }

- ry, hal - le - lu - jah, He reigns, _____ He reigns. __

|1. |2.

__ 2. Let it __ { It’s all God’s chil - dren sing - ing }
All God’s peo - ple sing - ing }

Chorus

glo - ry, glo - ry, hal - le - lu - jah, He reigns, _____

He reigns. {It's all God's chil - dren sing - ing / All God's peo - ple sing - ing} glo - ry, glo -

- ry, hal - le - lu - jah, He reigns, He reigns.

To Coda ⊕

Verse

3. And all the pow - ers of dark - ness trem - ble at what

they've just heard.

'Cause all the pow - ers of dark - ness can't drown out

a sin - gle word. When all God's chil - dren sing out

D.S. al Coda
(take 2nd ending)

⊕**Coda**

He reigns. All God's chil - dren sing - ing glo - ry, glo -

- ry, hal - le - lu - jah, He reigns.

Hands and Feet

**Words and Music by Mark Stuart, Will McGinniss,
Bob Herdman, Tyler Burkum and Charlie Peacock**

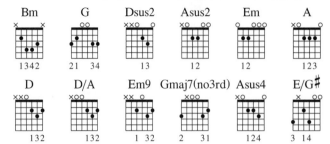

Strum Pattern: 3, 4
Pick Pattern: 3, 4

Verse
Moderately

1. An im-age flashed a-cross my T V screen, an-oth-er bro - ken heart comes
2. *See additional lyrics*

in - to view. I saw the pain and I turned my back.

Why can't I do the things I want to? I am will-ing, yet I'm

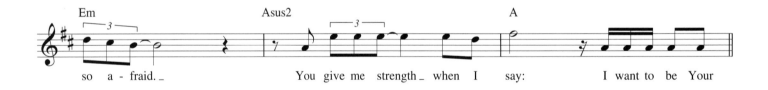

so a - fraid. You give me strength when I say: I want to be Your

Chorus

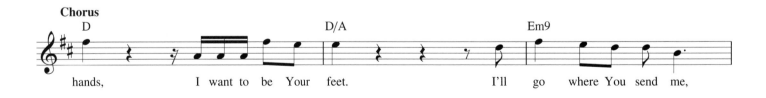

hands, I want to be Your feet. I'll go where You send me,

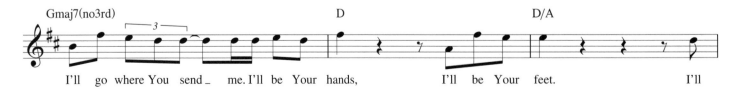

I'll go where You send me. I'll be Your hands, I'll be Your feet. I'll

go   where You send me,   I'll go where You send _ me. And I'll try,   yeah, I'll

try   to touch the world   like You touched my   life. ___   And I'll

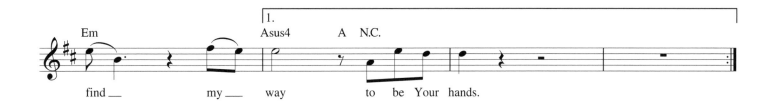

find ___   my ___ way   to be Your hands.

way. _____   This   is the last _ time   I   turn my back _ on You.

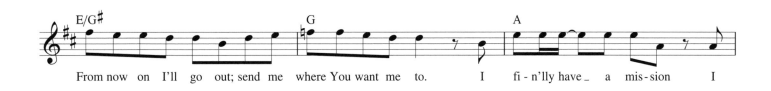

From now on I'll go out; send me where You want me to.   I   fi - n'lly have _ a mis - sion   I

prom- ise I'll ___ com- plete.   I   don't need ex - cus - es when I   am Your hands and feet.   I

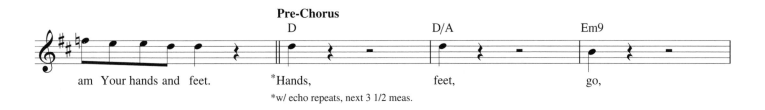

am Your hands and feet.   *Hands,   feet,   go,

*w/ echo repeats, next 3 1/2 meas.

Outro-Chorus

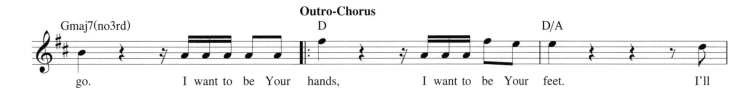

go.   I want to be Your   hands,   I want to be Your feet.   I'll

Repeat and fade

Additional Lyrics

2. I've abandoned ev'ry selfish thought,
   I've surrendered ev'rything I've got.
   You can have ev'rything I am,
   And perfect ev'rything I'm not.
   I am willing, I'm not afraid.
   You give me strength when I say:

He Walked a Mile

Words and Music by Dan Muckala

Strum Pattern: 7, 8
Pick Pattern: 7, 9

Verse
Moderately

1. Be - fore the __ threads of time be - gan, was pre - or - dained __ a might - y plan __
2. Feet so __ dust - y, cracked with heat, but car - ried on __ by love's heart - beat. __

that I should __ walk with Him a - lone, the cords of trust __ un - bro - ken.
A man of __ sor - rows filled with grief, for - give - ness was __ His an - them.

But fate fore - saw my wan - d'ring eye that none could yet re - strain;
No fee - ble blow from tongue or pen could ev - er __ sway my love for

His Eyes

Words and Music by Steven Curtis Chapman and James Isaac Elliott

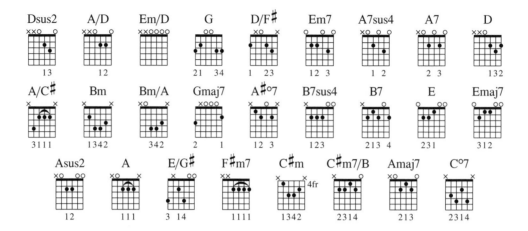

Strum Pattern: 2, 3
*Pick Pattern: 2, 4

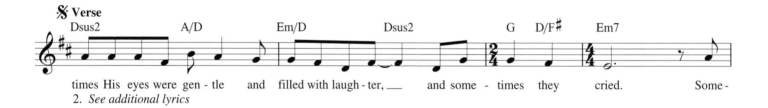

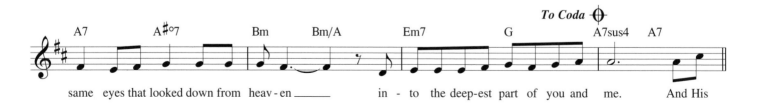

mat - ter where _ you go, you will al - ways be in His eyes

Outro

Some - times His eyes are gen - tle and filled with laugh - ter. _

Additional Lyrics

2. Sometimes His voice comes calling
   Like a rolling thunder, or like driving rain.
   And sometimes His voice is quiet
   And we start to wonder if He knows our pain.
   But He who spoke peace to the water
   Cares more for our hearts than the waves,
   And the voice that once said, "You're forgiven,"
   Still says, "You're forgiven," today, today.

How Great Is Our God

Words and Music by Chris Tomlin, Jesse Reeves and Ed Cash

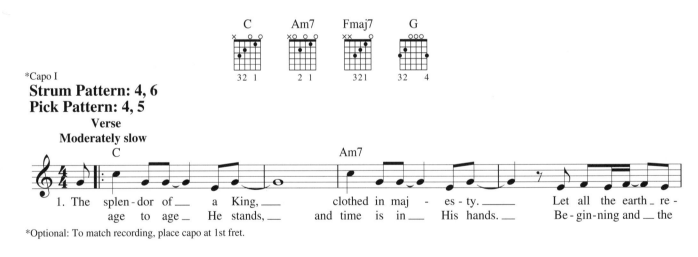

*Capo I
Strum Pattern: 4, 6
Pick Pattern: 4, 5

Verse
Moderately slow

1. The splen - dor of _ a King, _ clothed in maj - es - ty. _ Let all the earth _ re -
   age to age _ He stands, _ and time is in _ His hands. _ Be - gin - ning and _ the

*Optional: To match recording, place capo at 1st fret.

joice, all the earth _ re - joice. He wraps _ Him - self _ in light, _ and
end, be - gin - ning and _ the end. The God - head, three _ in one, _

dark - ness tries ___ to hide. ___ It trem - bles at ___ His voice, trem - bles at ___ His
Fa - ther, Spir - it, Son, ___ the Li - on and ___ the Lamb, Li - on and ___ the

Chorus

voice. }
Lamb. } How great ___ is our God! ___ Sing with me, _ how great ___ is our God! _

___ And all will see how great, how great ___ is our God! ___ 2. And

Bridge

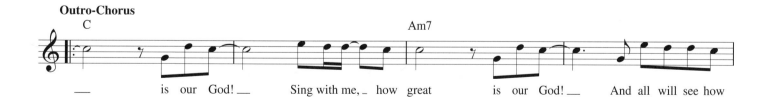

Name a - bove ___ all names, wor - thy of ___ all praise. My

heart will sing, _ "How great ___ is our God!" ___ How great

Outro-Chorus

___ is our God! ___ Sing with me, _ how great is our God! ___ And all will see how

great, how great ___ is our God! ___ How great ___

His Strength Is Perfect

Words and Music by Steven Curtis Chapman and Jerry Salley

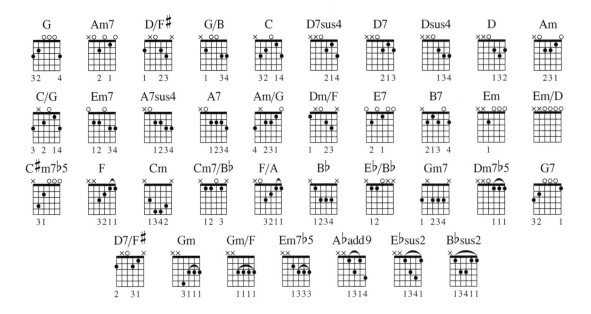

Strum Pattern: 1, 2
Pick Pattern: 2, 4

Intro
Moderately slow

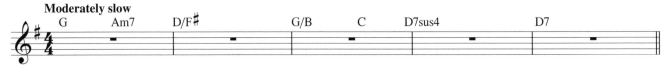

%. Verse

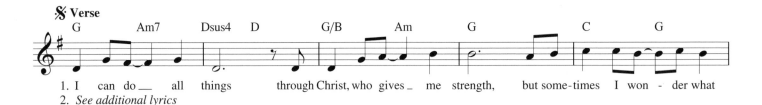

1. I can do ___ all things through Christ, who gives ___ me strength, but some-times I won - der what
2. *See additional lyrics*

He can do ___ through me. No great suc - cess ___ to show, no

glo - ry on ___ my own, yet in my weak-ness He ___ is there to let me know

Chorus

His strength is per - fect when our strength is gone. He'll car - ry

Additional Lyrics

2. We can only know the power that He holds
When we truly see how deep our weakness goes.
His strength in us begins when ours comes to an end.
He hears our humble cry and proves again...

Holy Is the Lord

Words and Music by Chris Tomlin and Louie Giglio

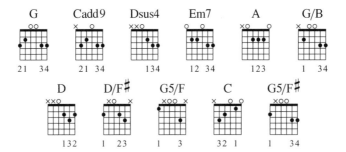

*Capo II
Strum Pattern: 1
Pick Pattern: 3

Verse
Moderately

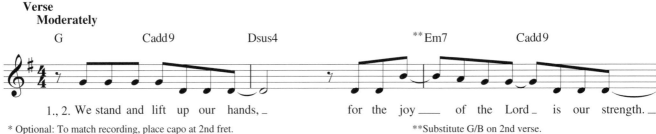

1., 2. We stand and lift up our hands, _ for the joy __ of the Lord _ is our strength. _

* Optional: To match recording, place capo at 2nd fret.   **Substitute G/B on 2nd verse.

__ We bow down __ and wor - ship Him now. __ How great, _

%. **Pre-Chorus**

***Em7

___ how awe - some is He. ___ And to - geth - er we sing. _____

***As before

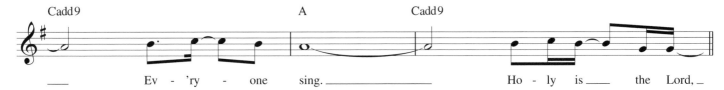

__ Ev - 'ry - one sing. _____ Ho - ly is ___ the Lord, _

Chorus

___ God _____ Al - might - y. _____ The earth ___ is filled _ with His glo -

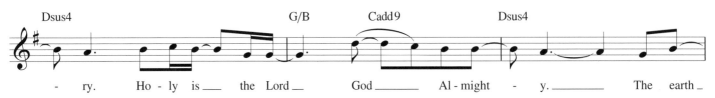

- ry. Ho - ly is __ the Lord _ God _____ Al - might - y. _____ The earth _

I Believe

Words and Music by Fran King and Wes King

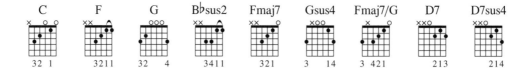

C   F   G   B♭sus2   Fmaj7   Gsus4   Fmaj7/G   D7   D7sus4

Strum Pattern: 4
Pick Pattern: 2

Verse
Moderately fast

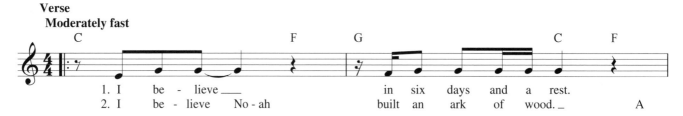

1. I be-lieve ___ in six days and a rest.
2. I be-lieve No-ah built an ark of wood. ___ A

God is good, I do con-fess. I be-lieve ___
hun-dred and twen-ty years, no one un-der-stood. I be-lieve ___ El-

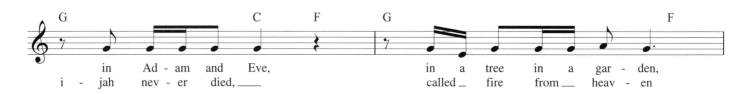

in Ad-am and Eve, in a tree in a gar-den,
i-jah nev-er died, ___ called ___ fire from ___ heav-en

𝄋 Chorus

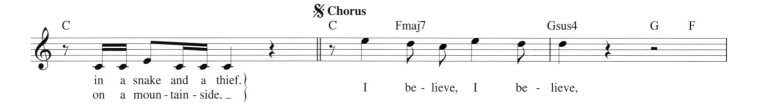

in a snake and a thief.)
on a moun-tain-side. ___)   I be-lieve, I be-lieve,

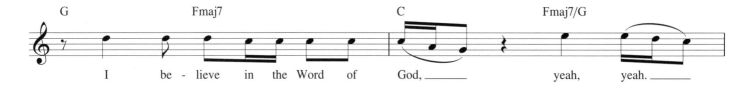

I be-lieve in the Word of God, ___ yeah, yeah.

To Coda ⊕

I be-lieve, I be-lieve, 'cause He made me be-

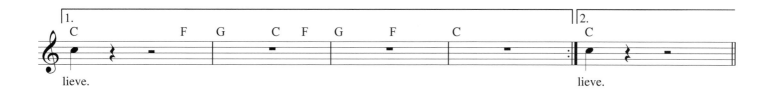

1. lieve.
2. lieve.

Bridge

It's been passed down through ag - es of time,

writ - ten by hands of men, in - spired by the Lord. His

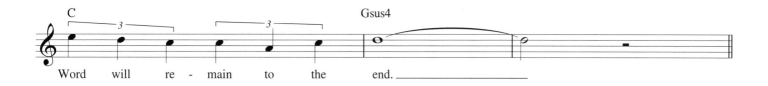

Word will re - main to the end.

Verse

3. I be - lieve I - sa - iah was a proph - et of old;

the Lamb was slain just as he fore - told. Well, I be - lieve Je - sus

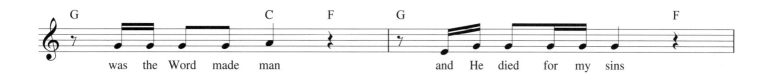

was the Word made man and He died for my sins

D.S. al Coda

Coda

and He rose a - gain. Don't you know that lieve.

I Can Only Imagine

Words and Music by Bart Millard

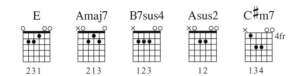

Strum Pattern: 1
Pick Pattern: 1

Intro
Moderately

Verse

1. I can on-ly im-ag-ine what it will be ___ like
2. *See additional lyrics*

when I walk ___ by Your side. I can on-ly im-

ag-ine what my eyes will see when Your face ___

is be-fore me. I can on-ly im-ag-ine.

Chorus

Sur-round-ed by ___ Your glo-ry what will my heart feel? ___ Will I

dance for You, Je - sus, or in awe of You _ be still? Will I stand in Your

pres - ence or to my knees will I fall? _ Will I sing hal - le - lu - jah? Will I be

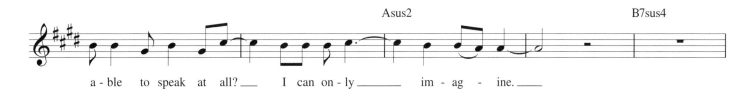

a - ble to speak at all? ___ I can on - ly _____ im - ag - ine. ____

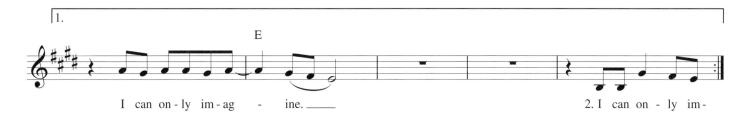

I can on - ly im - ag - ine. _____ 2. I can on - ly im -

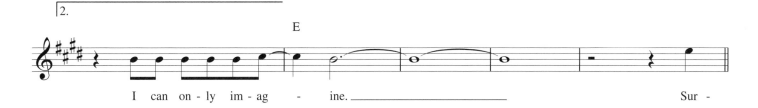

I can on - ly im - ag - ine. _____ Sur -

Chorus

round - ed by __ Your glo - ry, what will my heart feel? Will I dance for You, Je -

- sus, or in awe of You _ be still? Will I stand in Your pres - ence or to my

knees will I fall? Will I sing hal - le - lu - jah? ___ Will I be a - ble to speak at all? _

*Let chord ring, next 4 meas.

Outro

Additional Lyrics

2. I can only imagine when that day comes,
And I find myself standing in the Son.
I can only imagine when all I will do
Is forever, forever worship You.
I can only imagine.
I can only imagine.

I Still Believe

Words and Music by Jeremy Camp

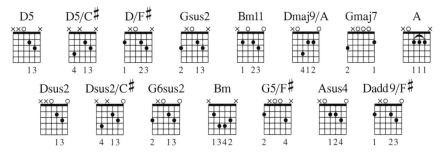

*Capo 1

Strum Pattern: 7, 8
Pick Pattern: 7, 8

Verse

Moderately

1. Scat-tered words and emp-ty thoughts seem to pour
2. Though the ques-tions still fog up my mind with prom-is-es I

*Optional: To match recording, place capo at 1st fret.

from my heart. I've nev-er felt so torn be - fore.
still seem to bear, or e-ven when an - swers slow-ly un - wind, it's

Seems I don't know where to start.
my heart I see You pre-pare.

Pre-Chorus

But it's now

that I feel Your grace fall like rain

from ev-'ry fin-ger-tip, wash-ing a-way my pain.

Chorus

'Cause I still be-lieve in Your

faith - ful - ness. _____ 'Cause I still be - lieve ___

in Your truth. _____ 'Cause I still be - lieve _

_____ in Your _ ho - ly Word. _____ E - ven when _

I don't see, _____ I still be - lieve. __

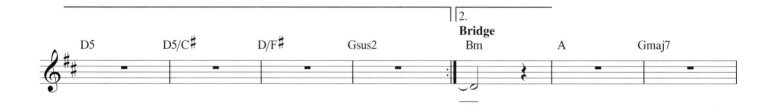

Well, the __ on - ly place _ I can go __ is in - to Your _ arms, __ where I ____ throw _

_____ to You _ my ___ fee - ble ___ prayers. _____ Well, in bro - ken - ness,

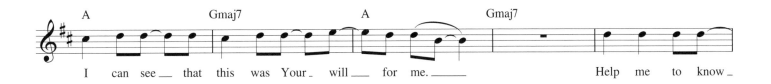

I can see _ that this was Your_ will _ for me. _____ Help me to know _

D.S. al Coda

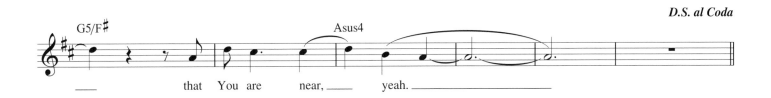

_ that You are near, _____ yeah. _____

⊕ Coda

Outro

_ 'cause I still be - lieve. _____ 'Cause I still be - lieve. _

_ 'Cause I still _ be - lieve. _____

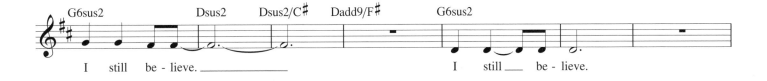

I still be - lieve. _____ I still _ be - lieve.

But I still be - lieve. _

I still be - lieve. _ I still be - lieve. _

I Will Be Here

Words and Music by Steven Curtis Chapman

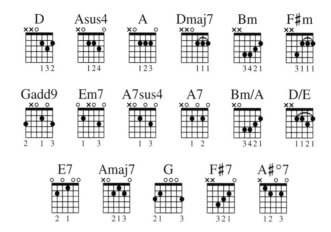

Strum Pattern: 3
Pick Pattern: 2

Verse
Slowly

1. To-mor-row morn-in' if you __ wake up and the sun does __ not __ ap - pear, __

2. *See additional lyrics*

I, _____ I will be here. __

If in the dark __ we __ lose sight __ of __ love, __ hold my __

__ hand and __ have __ no fear, 'cause I, _____

I will be here. ___ I will be here __

Chorus

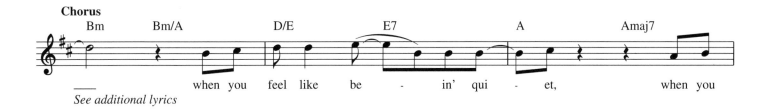

See additional lyrics

____ when you feel like be - in' qui - et, when you

need to speak ___ your ___ mind, ___ I ____ will lis - ten, and I will be here. __

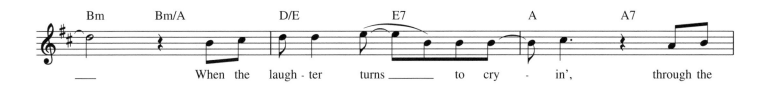

____ When the laugh - ter turns _____ to cry - in', through the

win - nin', los - in' and try - in', we'll be to - geth - er, _____

1.

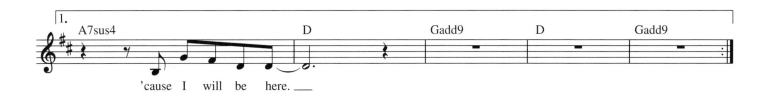

'cause I will be here. ___

2.   **Bridge**

Hmm. _____ I will ___ be ____ true to the prom -

- ise I ____ have _____ made to you and to _____ the One __

____ who gave you to _____ me.

Interlude

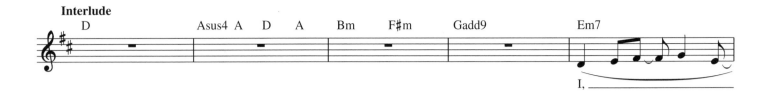

I,

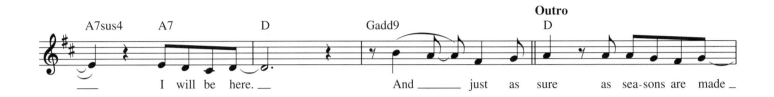

A7sus4   A7   D   Gadd9   **Outro** D

___   I will be here. ___   And ___ just as sure   as sea-sons are made ___

Asus4   A   D   Dmaj7   Bm   F♯m   Gadd9   D

___ for ___ change, ___   our life-times are made ___ for ___ years, ___   so

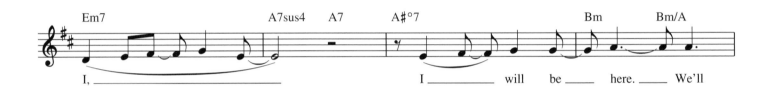

Em7   A7sus4   A7   A♯°7   Bm   Bm/A

I, ___   I ___ will   be ___ here. ___ We'll

Em7   A7sus4   A   D

be to - geth - er. ___   I   will   be ___ here. ___

Gadd9   D   Em7   A7sus4   D

Additional Lyrics

2. Tomorrow mornin', if you wake up and the future is unclear,
I will be here.
As sure as seasons are made for change,
Our lifetimes are made for years.
So I, I will be here.

Chorus I will be here and you can cry on my shoulder.
When the mirror tells us we're older,
I will hold you.
And I will be here to watch you grow in beauty
And tell you all the things you are to me.
I will be here.

If You Want Me To

Words and Music by Ginny Owens and Kyle Matthews

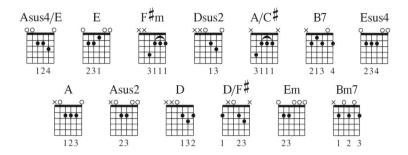

Strum Pattern: 3, 6
Pick Pattern: 3, 4

Verse
Reflectively

1. The path - way __ is bro - ken and the signs are __ un - clear. __ And __

__ I don't know the rea - son why You brought __ me here. __ But

just be - cause __ You love __ me __ the way that __ You __ do, I'm __ gon - na

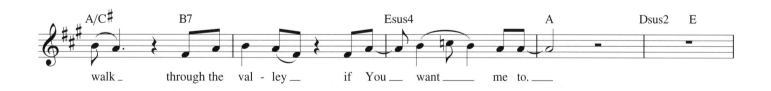

walk __ through the val - ley __ if You __ want __ me to. __

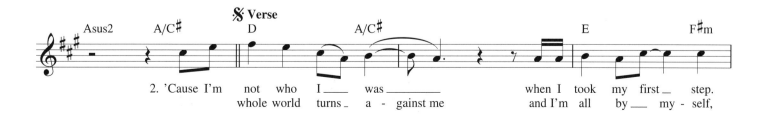

2. 'Cause I'm not who I __ was __ when I took my first __ step.
   whole world turns __ a - gainst me and I'm all by __ my - self,

And I'm ___ clin - in' to the prom - ise You're ___ not through with ___ me yet.
and I can't ___ hear ___ You an - swer my cries ___ for help,

So if all of these tri - als ___ bring me ___ close - er ___ to You, ___
I'll re - mem - ber the suf - f'ring. ___ that Your ___ love ___ put ___ You through. ___

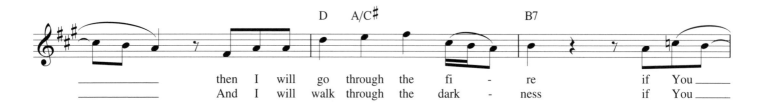

___ then I will go through the fi - re if You ___
___ And I will walk through the dark - ness if You ___

Interlude

To Coda ⊕

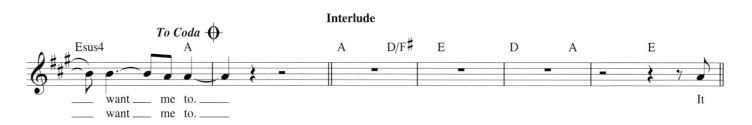

___ want ___ me to. ___
___ want ___ me to. ___

It

Bridge

may not be ___ the way ___ I ___ would have cho - sen, ___ when You

lead me through ___ a world ___ that's not my home.

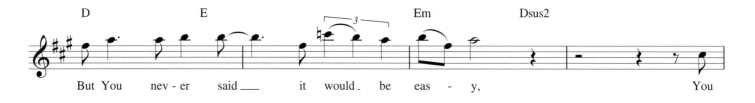

But You nev - er said ___ it would ___ be eas - y, You

on - ly said __ I'll nev - er go a - lone. 3. So when the

Coda

Verse

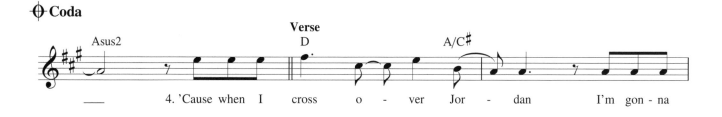

__ 4. 'Cause when I cross o - ver Jor - dan I'm gon - na

sing, gon-na shout. I'm gon-na look in - to __ Your eyes __ and see __ You

nev - er let __ me down. __ So take me on the path - way that

leads me home __ to You, and I will walk through the val - ley __ if You

want _____ me to. Yes, I will

walk through the val - ley __ if You __ want _____ me to.

In Heaven's Eyes

Words and Music by Phill McHugh

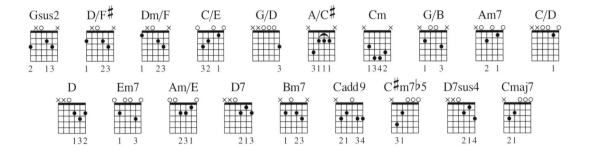

Strum Pattern: 2, 3
Pick Pattern: 4, 6

Verse

Moderately slow

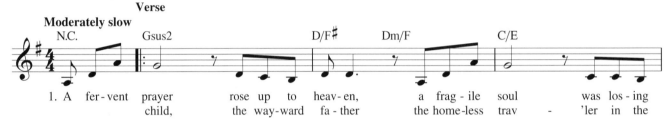

1. A fer-vent prayer rose up to heav-en, a frag-ile soul was los-ing
child, the way-ward fa-ther the home-less trav - 'ler in the

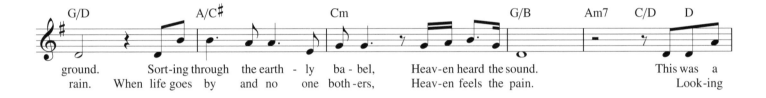

ground. Sort-ing through the earth - ly ba - bel, Heav-en heard the sound. This was a
rain. When life goes by and no one both-ers, Heav-en feels the pain. Look-ing

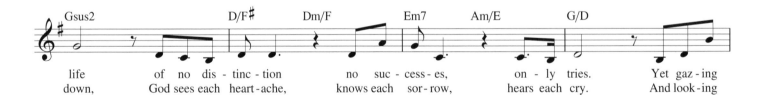

life of no dis - tinc - tion no suc - cess - es, on - ly tries. Yet gaz-ing
down, God sees each heart-ache, knows each sor - row, hears each cry. And look-ing

down on this un-love - ly one, ___ there was love ___ in Heav-en's eyes. ___
up we'll see com-pas - sion's fire, ___ a - blaze ___ in Heav-en's eyes. ___

% Chorus

In Heav-en's eyes, ___ there are no los-ers. In Heav-en's eyes, ___ no hope-less cause. ___

On-ly peo-ple like you with feel-ings like me, a-mazed by the grace we can find in Heav-en's

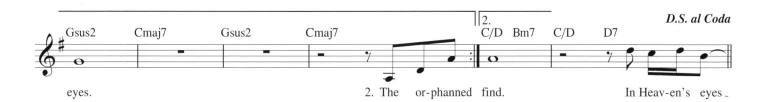

eyes. 2. The or-phaned find. In Heav-en's eyes _

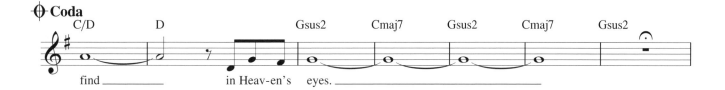

find _____ in Heav-en's eyes. _____

Let Us Pray

Words and Music by Steven Curtis Chapman

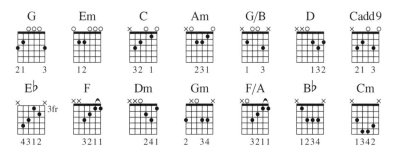

*Capo III

Strum Pattern: 1
Pick Pattern: 2

Verse
Moderately

1. I hear you say your heart is ach-ing, you've got trou-ble in the mak-ing, and you ask if I'll be
2. *See additional lyrics*

*To match recording, place capo at 3rd fret.

pray-ing for you, please. And in keep-ing with con - ven-tion, I'll say, "yes" with good in -

ten-tions to pray la - ter, mak-ing men-tion of your needs. But since we have this mo-ment

here at heav - en's door, we should start knock-ing now. _ What are we wait - ing for? Let us

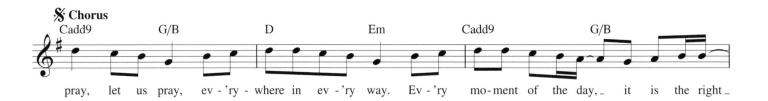

% Chorus

pray, let us pray, ev - 'ry - where in ev -'ry way. Ev - 'ry mo-ment of the day, _ it is the right _

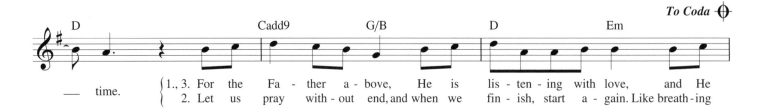

To Coda ⊕

_ time. 1., 3. For the Fa - ther a - bove, He is lis - ten-ing with love, and He
2. Let us pray with - out end, and when we fin - ish, start a - gain. Like breath-ing

1.

wants to an - swer us, _ so let us pray.

2. **Bridge**

out and breath-ing in, _ oh, let us pray. Let us ap - proach _ the throne of grace with con -

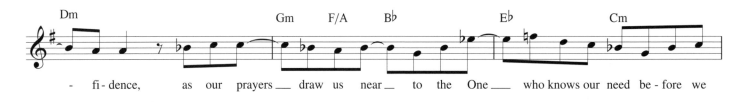

- fi - dence, as our prayers _ draw us near _ to the One _ who knows our need be - fore we

D.S. al Coda ⊕ **Coda** **Chorus**

e - ven call His name. Let us wants to an - swer us. _ Oh, let us pray, let us pray, ev - 'ry -

where and ev - 'ry way. Ev - 'ry mo-ment of the day, _ it is the right _ time. And let us

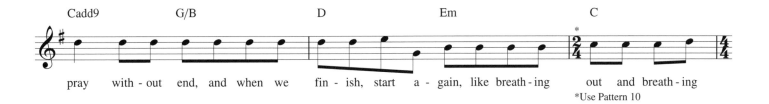

pray   with-out   end,   and   when   we   fin-ish,   start   a-gain,   like   breath-ing   out   and   breath-ing

*Use Pattern 10

in,   whoa,   let   us   pray.   Oh,   let   us   pray, _____   yeah. ___

1.   2.   **Outro**

___   Let   us   ___   Pray   this   way: Our   Fa-ther which art ___   in   heav-en,

hal-low-ed   be Thy   name. _   Thy   king-dom come, _ Thy   will   be   done on earth,   as   it   is   in   heav-en.

N.C.

Let   us   pray.   Let   us   pray,   let   us   pray,   oh,   let   us   pray,   yeah. ___

Additional Lyrics

2. So when you feel the Spirit moving,
    Prompting, prodding and behooving,
    There is no time to be losing,
    Let us pray.
    Let the Father hear us saying
    What we need to be conveying.
    Even while this song is playing,
    Let us pray.
    And just because we say the word, "Amen,"
    It doesn't mean this conversation needs to end.

In the Blink of an Eye

Words and Music by Bart Millard, Nathan Cochran, Mike Scheuchzer,
Jim Bryson, Robby Shaffer, Barry Graul and Peter Kipley

Strum Pattern: 1, 2
Pick Pattern: 2, 4

Verse
Moderately

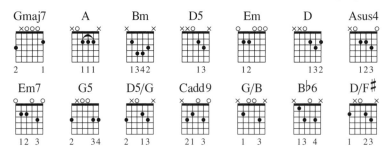

1. You put me here for a rea - son. You have a mis-sion for me. ___

You knew my name and You called ___ it long be - fore ___ I learned ___ to breathe.

Verse

2. Some-times I feel dis-ap-point - ed by the way ___ I spend ___ my time. ___
3. And though I'm liv - ing a good ___ life, can my life ___ be some - thing great? ___

How can I fur-ther Your king - dom when I'm so ___ wrapped up ___ in mine? ___
I have to an-swer the ques - tion be - fore ___ it's too ___ late, ___

Chorus

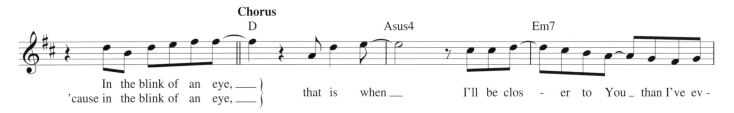

In the blink of an eye, ___ } that is when ___ I'll be clos - er to You ___ than I've ev -
'cause in the blink of an eye, ___ }

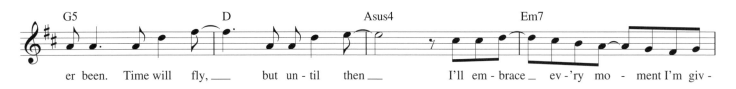

er been. Time will fly, ___ but un - til then ___ I'll em - brace ev - 'ry mo - ment I'm giv -

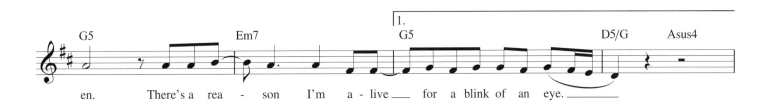

en. There's a rea - son I'm a - live___ for a blink of an eye.___

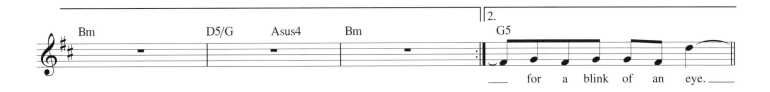

for a blink of an eye.___

Bridge

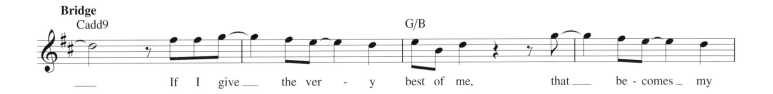

___ If I give___ the ver - y best of me, that___ be - comes___ my

leg - a - cy, so tell me, what___ am I wait - ing for? ___ What___

Outro-Chorus

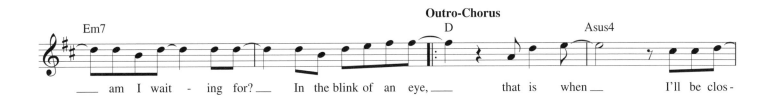

___ am I wait - ing for?___ In the blink of an eye, ___ that is when___ I'll be clos -

- er to You___ than I've ev - er been. Time will fly,___ but un - til then___ I'll em - brace___

___ ev - 'ry mo - ment I'm giv - en. In the blink of an eye,___ en. There's a rea - son I'm a - live___

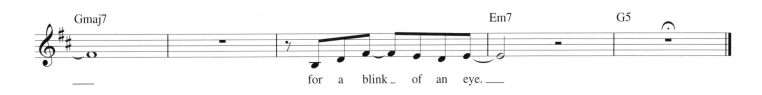

___ for a blink___ of an eye.___

Jesus Freak

Words and Music by Toby McKeehan and Mark Heimermann

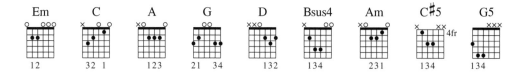

Strum Pattern: 1
Pick Pattern: 2, 5

Verse
Moderately

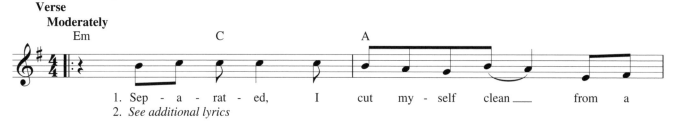

1. Sep - a - rat - ed, I cut my - self clean ___ from a
2. *See additional lyrics*

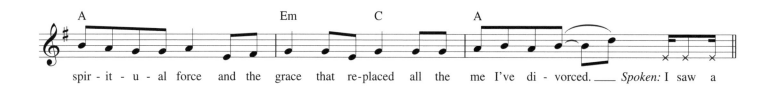

past that comes back in my dark - est of dreams. ___ Been ap - pre - hend - ed by a

spir - it - u - al force and the grace that re - placed all the me I've di - vorced. ___ *Spoken:* I saw a

Pre-Chorus

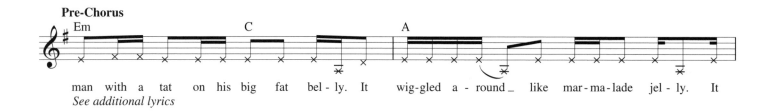

man with a tat on his big fat bel - ly. It wig - gled a - round ___ like mar - ma - lade jel - ly. It
See additional lyrics

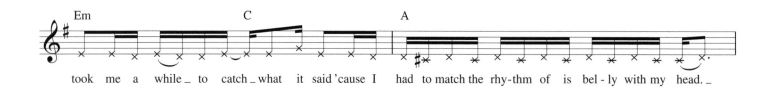

took me a while ___ to catch ___ what it said 'cause I had to match the rhy - thm of is bel - ly with my head. ___

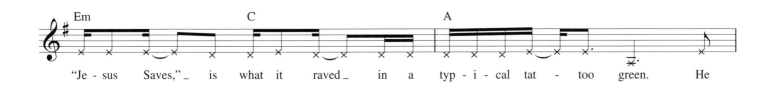

"Je - sus Saves," _ is what it raved _ in a typ - i - cal tat - too green. He

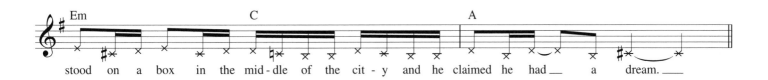

stood on a box in the mid - dle of the cit - y and he claimed he had __ a dream. __

%· Chorus

What will peo - ple think _ when they hear that I'm _ a Je - sus freak? What will peo - ple do ___ when they

find that it's true? _ I don't real - ly care ___ if they la - bel me a Je - sus freak.

To Coda ⊕ ⌐1.

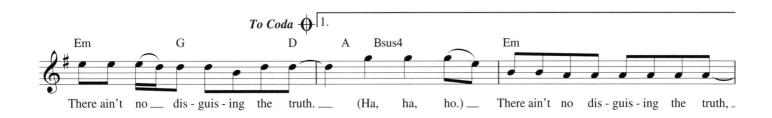

There ain't no __ dis - guis - ing the truth. ___ (Ha, ha, ho.) ___ There ain't no dis - guis - ing the truth, _

⌐2.   *D.S. al Coda*

___ though I ain't in - to hid - ing _____ the truth. ___ (Ha, ha, ho.) ___

⊕ **Coda**   **Interlude**

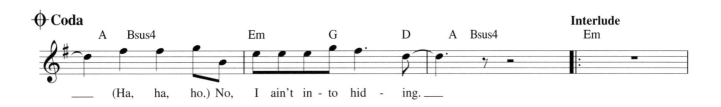

___ (Ha, ha, ho.) No, I ain't in - to hid - ing. ___

Bridge

Play 4 times

Peo - ple say I'm strange, does it ___ make me a stran - ger that

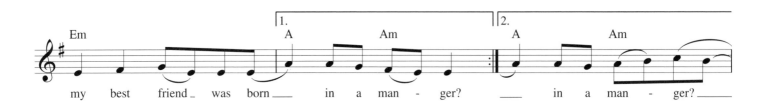

my best friend ___ was born ___ in a man - ger? ___ in a man - ger? ___

Guitar Solo

Outro-Chorus

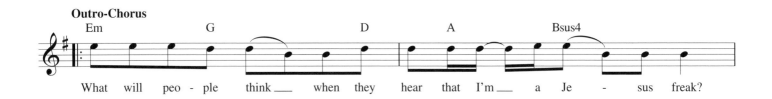

What will peo - ple think ___ when they hear that I'm ___ a Je - sus freak?

What will peo - ple do ___ when they find that it's true? ___ I don't real - ly care ___ if they

Repeat and fade

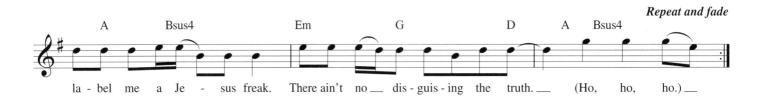

la - bel me a Je - sus freak. There ain't no ___ dis - guis - ing the truth. ___ (Ho, ho, ho.) ___

Additional Lyrics

2. Kamikaze, my death is gain.
I've been marked by my Maker a peculiar display, yeah, ah.
(Peculiar display.)
The high and lofty, they see me as weak
'Cause I won't live and die for the power they seek, yeah.

Pre-Chorus Spoken: There was a man from the desert with naps in his head.
The sand that he walked was also his bed,
The words that he spoke made the people assume
There wasn't too much left in the upper room.
With skins on his back and hair on his face,
They thought he was strange by the locusts he ate.
You see the Pharisees tripped when they heard him speak
Until the king took the head of this Jesus freak.

Live Out Loud

Words and Music by Steven Curtis Chapman and Geoff Moore

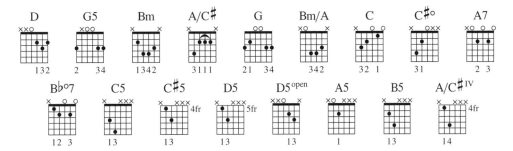

*Tune down 1/2 step:
(low to high) E♭–A♭–D♭–G♭–B♭–E♭

Strum Pattern: 1
Pick Pattern: 4

Intro
Moderately

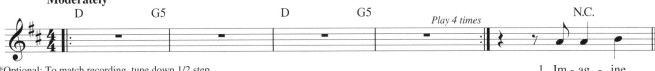

*Optional: To match recording, tune down 1/2 step.

1. Im - ag - ine

Verse

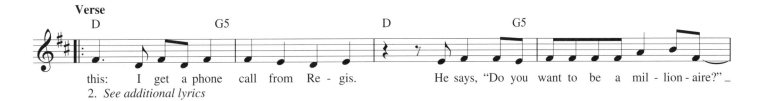

this: I get a phone call from Re - gis.   He says, "Do you want to be a mil - lion - aire?"_
2. *See additional lyrics*

___ They put me on the show and I win with two life - lines to spare.   Now, pic - ture

this: I act like noth-ing ev - er hap - pened   and bur - y all the mon - ey in a cof - fee can._

___ Well, I've been giv - en more than Re - gis ev - er gave a - way.___ I was a

dead man who was called to come out from my___ grave.___ And I think it's time for

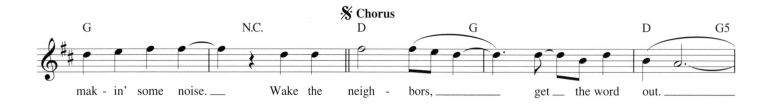

mak - in' some noise. ___ Wake the neigh - bors, _____ get ___ the word out. _____

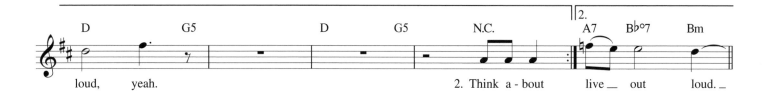

___ Come on, crank up the mu - sic, climb a moun - tain and shout. ___ This is

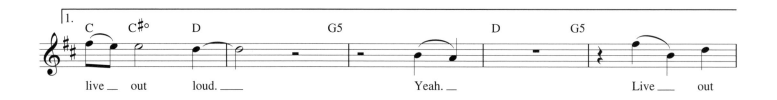

life we've been giv - en, made to be lived out, ___ so la, la, la, la,

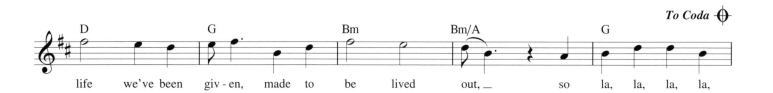

live ___ out loud. ___ Yeah. ___ Live ___ out

loud, yeah. 2. Think a - bout live ___ out loud. ___

___ Live out

loud. _____ Ev - 'ry - bod - y. La, la, la,

la, la, la, la, la, la, la, live out loud. ___

La, la, la, la, la, la, la, la, la, la,

live out loud.

Bridge
D5 ^{open}

Ev-'ry cor - ner of cre - a - tion

is a liv - ing de - clar - a - tion. Come join the song we were made to sing.

Coda

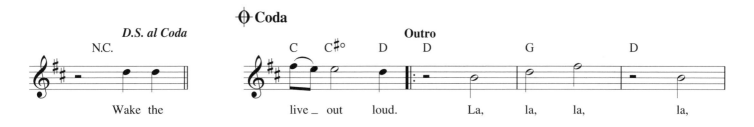

D.S. al Coda

Wake the

Outro

live out loud. La, la, la, la,

Repeat and fade

la, la, la, la, la, la, live out loud.

Additional Lyrics

2. Think about this:
   Try to keep a bird from singing
   After it's soared up in the sky,
   Give the sun a cloudless day
   And tell it not to shine.
   Now, think about this:
   If we really have been given
   The gift of life that will never end,
   And if we have been filled with living hope,
   We're gonna overflow,
   And if God's love is burning in our hearts,
   We're gonna know.
   There's just no way to keep it in.

Just One

Words and Music by Connie Harrington and Jim Cooper

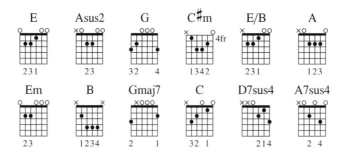

Strum Pattern: 6
Pick Pattern: 4

Intro
Free-spirited Rock

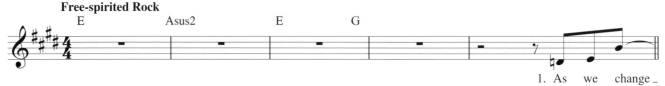

1. As we change

Verse

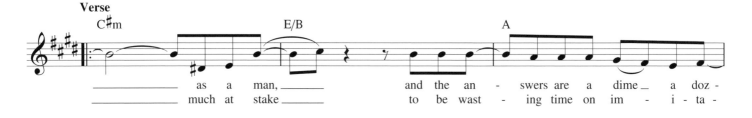

_____ as a man, _____ and the an - swers are a dime a doz-
_____ much at stake _____ to be wast - ing time on im - i - ta-

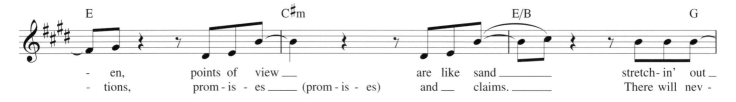

- en, points of view ___ are like sand _____ stretch - in' out
- tions, prom - is - es ___ (prom - is - es) and ___ claims. _____ There will nev-

___ as far ___ as the eye ___ can see. There's a thou - sand dif - f'rent phi - los-
- er be ___ a ___ sub - sti - tute for the blood, ___ the Word, ___ and the sim-

Chorus

- o - phies, but there's just ___ one book, ___ and there's just ___ one name with the pow-
- ple truth, 'cause there's just ___ one book, ___ and there's just ___ one name with the pow-

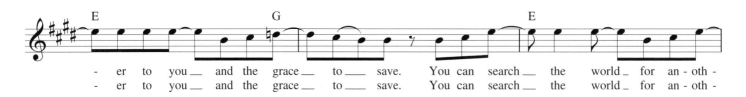

- er to you ___ and the grace ___ to ___ save. You can search ___ the world ___ for an - oth-
- er to you ___ and the grace ___ to ___ save. You can search ___ the world ___ for an - oth-

- er way, but if you're look - in' for the road to be - yond, _____ there's just _____ one.
- er way, but if you're look - in' for the road to be - yond, _

2. There's just too _____ _____ there's just _____ one door _____ to o - pen, where truth _
(door) _____

_____ and hope _____ will be wait - ing there _____ on the oth - er side. _____ Just _
_____ (on the oth - er side) _____

_____ one sto - ry that's nev - er end - ing with life _____ be - gin - ning in Je -

Interlude

- sus Christ, _____ yeah. _____

Outro-Chorus

You can search _____ the world _ for an - oth - er way, but if you're

look - in' for the road to be - yond, _ there's just _____ one, just _____ one book, _ and there's just _

Repeat and fade

_____ one name with the pow - er to heal _ and the grace _____ to _____ save. You can search _

Lifesong

Words and Music by Mark Hall

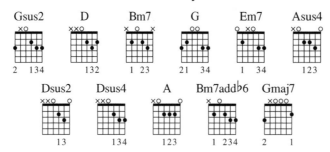

*Tune down 1/2 step:
(low to high) E♭–A♭–D♭–G♭–B♭–E♭

Strum Pattern: 4, 6
Pick Pattern: 4, 6

Verse

Moderately

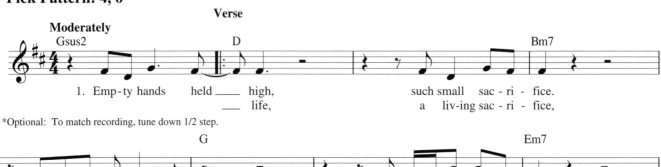

1. Emp-ty hands held ___ high, such small sac-ri-fice.
___ life, a liv-ing sac-ri-fice,

*Optional: To match recording, tune down 1/2 step.

If not joined ___ with my life, I sing in vain ___ to-night.
to reach a ___ world in need, to be Your hands ___ and feet.

May the words I say and the things I do make my life-song

Chorus

sing, bring a smile to You. Let my life-song

sing to You. ___ Let my life-song sing to You. ___

___ I want to sing Your name ___ to the end of this day, know-ing

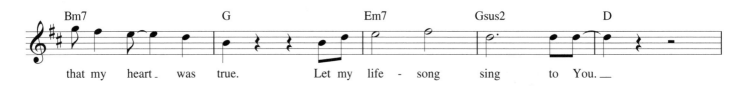

that my heart ___ was true. Let my life-song sing to You. ___

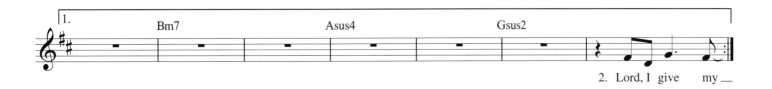

1.

Bm7   Asus4   Gsus2

2. Lord, I give my __

2.   **Bridge**

Gmaj7   D   Bm7   A

Hal - le - lu - jah! __ Hal - le - lu - jah! ____ Let my __

G   A   Bm7   Asus4   G

life - song sing to You. __ Hal - le - lu - jah! __

D   Bm7   A   G   A   Bm7

__ Hal - le - lu - jah! __ Let my __ life - long sing to You. __

Outro-Chorus

A   D   Dsus2   Dsus4   A

__ Let my life - song sing to You. __

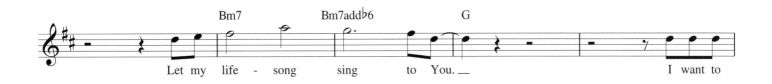

Bm7   Bm7add♭6   G

Let my life - song sing to You. __ I want to

A   Bm7

sing Your name __ to the end of this day, know-ing that my heart __ was

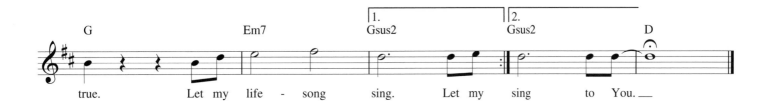

G   Em7   1. Gsus2   2. Gsus2   D

true. Let my life - song sing. Let my sing to You. __

A Little More

Words and Music by Jennifer Knapp

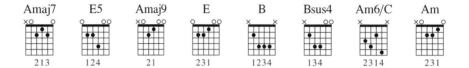

Strum Pattern: 6
Pick Pattern: 4

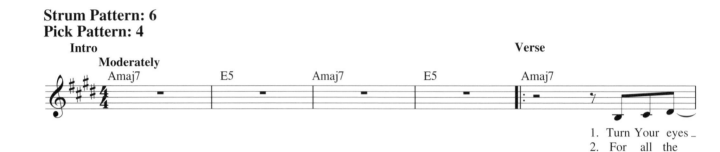

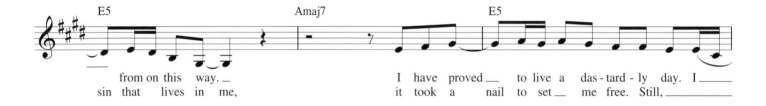

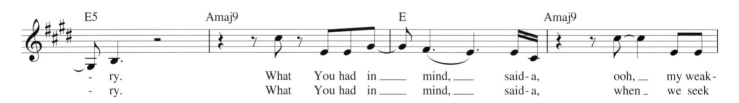

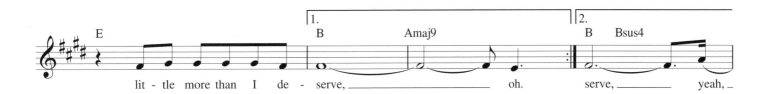

Bridge

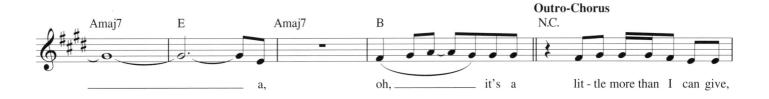

Outro-Chorus

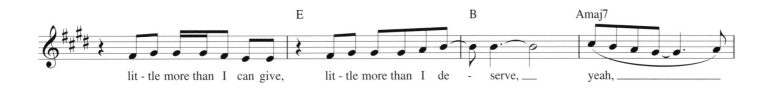

Love Will Be Our Home

Words and Music by Steven Curtis Chapman

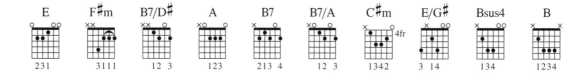

Strum Pattern: 1
Pick Pattern: 1

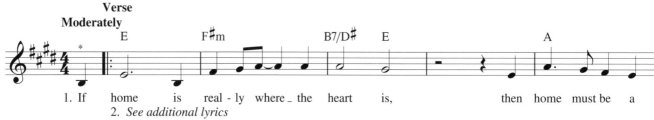

1. If home is real-ly where _ the heart is, then home must be a

Sung one octave higher than written.

2. *See additional lyrics*

place we all can share. For e-ven with _ our dif-f'renc-es, our hearts are much _ the

same. For where love is, _ we come to-geth-er there. _____ Wher-ev-er there _ is laugh-

-ter ring-ing, some-one smil-ing, _ some-one dream-ing, _ we can live _ to-geth-

-er there, _ love will be _____ our home.

{ Wher-ev-er there ___ are chil-
{ Where there are words _ of kind-

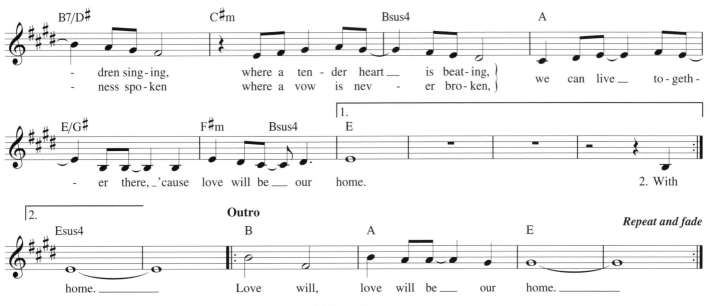

- dren sing-ing,   where a ten - der heart ___ is beat-ing,   we can live ___ to - geth -
- ness spo-ken   where a vow is nev - er bro-ken,

- er there, ___ 'cause love will be ___ our home.

2. With

2.

Outro

Repeat and fade

home. ___   Love will,   love will be ___ our home. ___

Additional Lyrics

2. With love, our hearts can be a family,
And hope can bring this family face to face.
And though we may be far apart,
Our hearts can beat as one
When love brings us together in one place.

Meant to Live

Words and Music by Jonathan Foreman and Tim Foreman

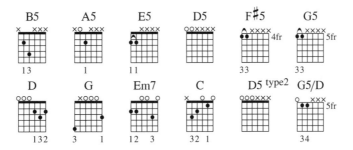

Drop D tuning:
(low to high) D–A–D–G–B–E

Strum Pattern: 2, 3

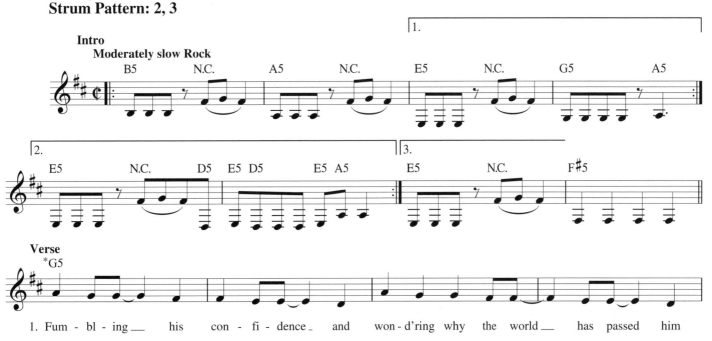

Intro
Moderately slow Rock

1. Fum - bl - ing ___ his con - fi - dence ___ and won - d'ring why the world ___ has passed him

*Play chord once and hold through next 4 measures.

by. _____

*G5

Hop - ing   that   he's   bent   for   more _   than   ar - gu - ments _   and   failed   at - tempts _   to

*As before

D5

fly, _____   fly. _____

𝄋 Chorus

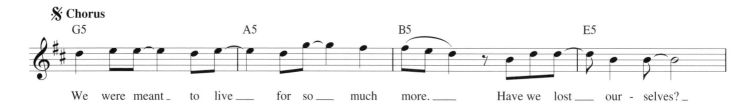

G5   A5   B5   E5

We   were   meant _   to   live ___   for   so ___   much   more. ___   Have   we   lost ___   our - selves? _

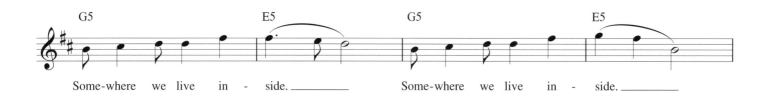

G5   E5   G5   E5

Some-where   we   live   in - side. _____   Some-where   we   live   in - side. _____

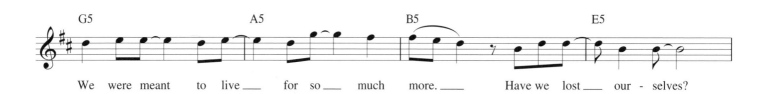

G5   A5   B5   E5

We   were   meant   to   live ___   for   so ___   much   more. ___   Have   we   lost ___   our - selves?

To Coda ⊕   **Interlude**

G5   E5   D5

Some-where   we   live   in - side. _____

Verse

*G5   D5

2. Dream-ing a-bout prov - i - dence _ and wheth-er mice and men _ have sec-ond tries. _
*As before

*G5

May - be we've been liv - in' with our eyes half o - pen. May - be we're bent and bro - ken,
*As before

D5

bro - ken.

D.S. al Coda

⊕ **Coda**

Interlude

E5   B5   N.C.

side.

A5   N.C.   E5   N.C.   D5   E5   D5

B5   N.C.   A5   N.C.   E5   N.C.

Bridge

F#5   D   G

We want more _____ than this world's _ got to of - fer.

We want more ___ than this world's ___ got to of - fer.

We want more ___ than the wars ___ of our fa - thers. And

ev -'ry - thing in - side screams for sec-ond life. Yeah. ___

Outro-Chorus

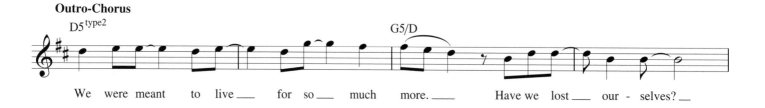

We were meant to live ___ for so ___ much more. ___ Have we lost ___ our - selves? ___

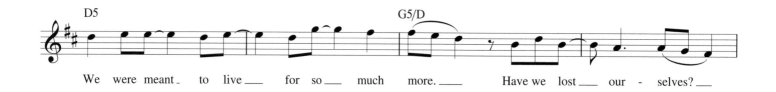

We were meant ___ to live ___ for so ___ much more. ___ Have we lost ___ our - selves? ___

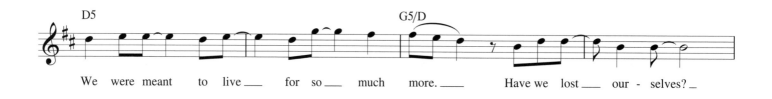

We were meant to live ___ for so ___ much more. ___ Have we lost ___ our - selves? ___

We were meant to live, ___ we were meant ___ to live. ___

Magnificent Obsession

Words and Music by Steven Curtis Chapman

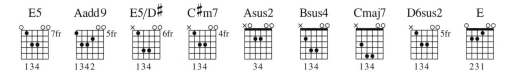

*Tune down 1/2 step:
(low to high) Eb–Ab–Db–Gb–Bb–Eb

Strum Pattern: 1
Pick Pattern: 3

Verse

Moderately

1. Lord, You know ___ how much ___ I want to know ___ so much ___ in the way ___
2. *See additional lyrics*

*Optional: To match recording, tune down 1/2 step.

___ of an - swers and ex - pla - na - tions. I have cried and ___ prayed, ___

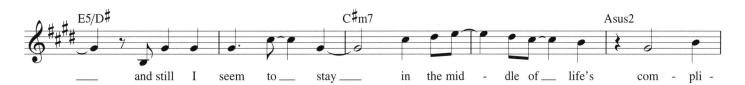

___ and still I seem to stay ___ in the mid - dle of ___ life's com - pli -

Pre-Chorus

ca - tions. All this pur - su - ing leaves me feel - ing like ___ I'm chas - ing down the wind, ___
See additional lyrics

___ but now it's brought ___ me back to You, ___ and I can see a - gain.

𝄋 Chorus

{1, 2. This is}
{3. You are} ev - 'ry - thing I want. {This is}
{You are} ev - 'ry - thing I need.

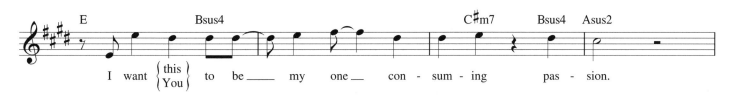

I want {this}{You} to be ___ my one ___ con - sum - ing pas - sion.

Chorus

'Cause You are ev - 'ry - thing _ I want. _ You are ev -'ry-thing I need.

I want You to be ____ my one ____ con - sum - ing pas - sion.

Ev - 'ry - thing ____ my _ heart _ de - sires, Lord, I want it all ____ to be _

____ for _____ You, ____ Je - sus. Be my mag - nif - i - cent _ ob - ses -

- sion. _____ Be my mag - nif - i - cent ob - ses - sion. _

Additional Lyrics

2. So capture my heart again.
Take me to depths I've never been,
Into the riches of Your grace and Your mercy.
Return me to the cross
And let me be completely lost
In the wonder of the love that You've shown me.

Pre-Chorus Cut through these chains that tie me down
To so many lesser things.
Let all my dreams fall to the ground
Until this one remains.

Mercy Came Running

Words and Music by Dan Dean, Dave Clark and Don Koch

Chorus

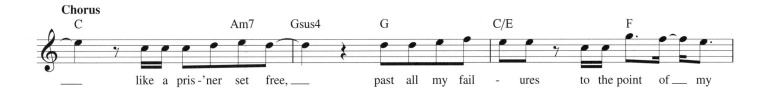

like a pris-'ner set free, ___ past all my fail - ures to the point of ___ my

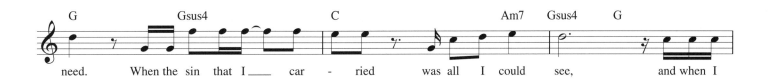

need. When the sin that I ___ car - ried was all I could see, and when I

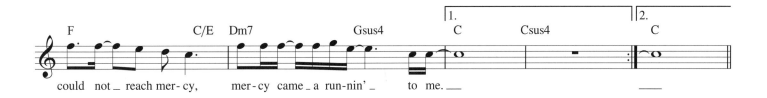

could not ___ reach mer- cy, mer- cy came ___ a run-nin' ___ to me. ___

Bridge

Some - times I still feel so far, so far from where ___ I real - ly should be.

He gent - ly calls to my heart ___ just to re-mind ___ me... Mer-cy came ___ a run-nin' ___

Chorus

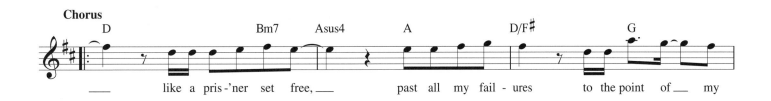

like a pris -'ner set free, ___ past all my fail - ures to the point of ___ my

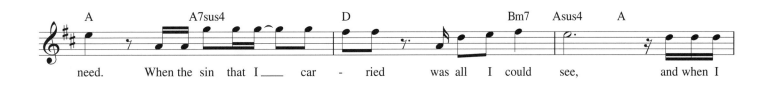

need. When the sin that I ___ car - ried was all I could see, and when I

could not ___ reach mer- cy, mer-cy came, ___ mer-cy came ___ a run-nin' ___ mer-cy came ___ a run-nin' ___ to me. ___

Million Pieces

Words and Music by Peter Furler and Steve Taylor

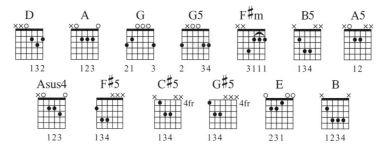

Strum Pattern: 2, 5
Pick Pattern: 1, 2

Intro
Moderately

Do, do, do, do.

Do, do, do, do.   Do, do, do, do.

% Chorus

Oh, they all fall like a mil - lion rain - drops

fall - ing from a blue sky kiss - in' your cares good - bye. _____

Oh, ___ as they all fall like a mil - lion piec - es, a

tick - er - tape ___ pa - rade ___ high, and now you're free ___ to fly. ___

To Coda ⊕
Verse

1. I'm car-ry-in' a mill-stone _ ma-laise. _____ It's been
2. *See additional lyrics*

pull-ing down _ your gaze. _____ You pound the pave - ment. It don't give or care, _ this

weight ain't yours _ to bear. _____ Why you hold - in' grudg - es in old ____ jars? ____

_ Why you wan - na show off all ____ your scars? _____ What's it gon - na

2nd time, D.S. al Coda

take to lay ____ a few bur - dens down? _ It's a beau - ti - ful sound _ when they

⊕ **Coda**
Bridge

You got - ta lay that bur - den down. _ You got - ta

lay that bur - den down. _ It's time to leave your bur - dens in a pyre, _

set a bon - fire. 'Cause when you lay your bur - dens down, _ when you

Additional Lyrics

2. When that muffled sigh
   Says you're barely getting by,
   Cut your burdens loose
   And just simplify, simplify.
   This is not your floor,
   You're going higher than before.
   Drop the weight now,
   Wait for the lookout guide.
   Look outside as they...

Mountain of God

Words and Music by Mac Powell and Brown Bannister

Strum Pattern: 4
Pick Pattern: 1

Verse
Moderately slow

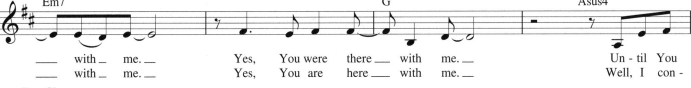

1. I thought that I ____ was all ____ a - lone, bro - ken and ___ a - fraid, ____
as I trav - el on ____ the road that You have led ___ me down, ____

____ but You were _ there ___ with me. ___ Yes, You were there ___ with me.
____ You are ___ here ___ with me. ___ Yes, You are here ___ with me. And

And I did - n't e - ven know ___ that I had lost ___ my way, ___ but You were _ there
I have need _ for noth - ing more, ___ oh, now that I ____ have found _ that You are ___ here

____ with _ me. ___ Yes, You were there ___ with me. Un - til You
____ with _ me. ___ Yes, You are here ___ with me. ___ Well, I con -

Pre-Chorus

o - pened up ___ my eyes, ___ I nev - er knew ____ that I
fess, from time _ to time ___ I lose ___ my way. ____ but You are

could - n't ev - er make ___ it with - out You. ___ }
al - ways there _ to bring ___ me back _ a - gain. ___ }
And e - ven though the

Chorus

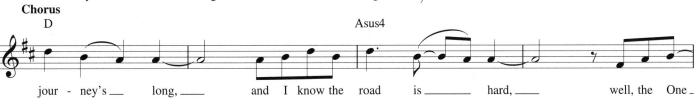

jour - ney's ___ long, ___ and I know the road is ___ hard, ___ well, the One

who's gone before me, He will help me carry on.

And after all that I've been through, well, now I realize the truth,

that I must go through the valley to stand

1. upon the mountain of God. 2. And upon the moun-

Bridge

tain of God. Sometimes I think of where it is I've come

from, and the things I've left behind.

But of all I've had, what I've possessed, nothing

can quite compare with what's in front of me, with what's in front

of me. Yeah, yeah. Even though the

Chorus

E5 · · · Bsus4

jour - ney's long, _____ and I know the road is _____ hard, _____ yeah, the One _

F♯m7add4 · · · Asus2

_ who's gone _ be - fore me, _____ He will help _____ me car - ry on. _____

Bsus4 · · · E5 · · · Bsus4

_____ And af - ter all that I've been through, _ now I re - al - ize the _ truth, _

F♯m7add4 · · · Asus2

_____ that I must _ go through _ the val - ley _____ to stand _ up - on _____ the moun-

Bsus4 · · · F♯m7add4 · · · Asus2

- tain. Yes, I must _ go through _ the val - ley to stand _ up - on _____ the moun-

Bsus4 · · · F♯m7add4 · · · Asus2

- tain. Yes, I must _ go through _ the val - ley to stand _ up - on _____ the moun-

Bsus4 · · · **Outro** · *E5

- tain. _____ I thought that I _ was all _
*One strum to end.

Bsus4

_____ a - lone, bro - ken and _ a - fraid, _____ but You are _ here _

F♯m7add4 · · · Asus2

_ with me. _ Yes, You are here _ with me. _

115

My Will

Words and Music by Toby McKeehan, Michael Tait, Joey Elwood and Daniel Pitts

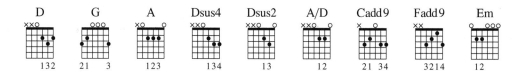

Strum Pattern: 6, 2
Pick Pattern: 4, 5

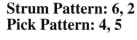

1. I'm set-ting the stage ___ for the things I love, ___ and I'm now the man ___
2., 3. *See additional lyrics*

___ I once could-n't be. And noth-ing on earth ___ could now ev - er

move me, I now have the will ___ and ___ the strength a man ___ needs. ___ It's my will, ___

Chorus

___ I'm not mov - ing, ___ 'cause if it's Your ___ will then noth-ing can shake ___

___ me. And it's my will ___ to bow and praise You. ___ I now have the

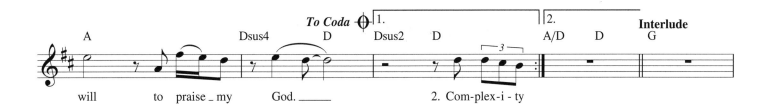

will to praise _ my God. _____ 2. Com-plex-i - ty

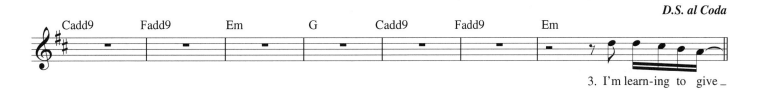

3. I'm learn-ing to give _

We've got _ to be chil - dren _ of peace. Don't you know,

we've got _ to be chil - dren _ of peace. _ And it's my will, _

_ I'm not mov - ing, _ 'cause if it's Your _ will then noth-ing can shake _

_ me. And it's my will _ to bow and praise You. _ I now have the

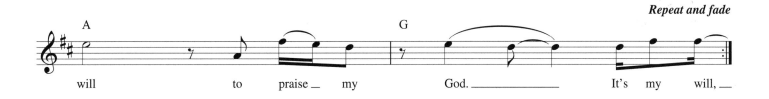

will to praise _ my God. _____ It's my will, _

Additional Lyrics

2. Complexity haunts me for I am two men,
Entrenched in a battle that I'll never win.
My discipline fails me, my knowledge, it fools me,
But You are my shelter, all the strength that I need.

3. I'm learning to give up the rights to myself,
The bits and the pieces I've gathered as wealth.
They'd never compare to the joy that You bring me,
The peace that You show me is the strength that I need.

Ocean Floor

Words and Music by Mark Stuart, Will McGinniss, Bob Herdman, Tyler Burkum and Ben Cissell

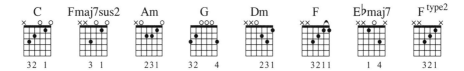

Strum Pattern: 2, 4
Pick Pattern: 4, 5

Intro
Moderately slow

Verse

1. The mis-takes I've made ___ that caused pain, ___ I could have

done with out. ___ All my self-ish thoughts, all my pride, ___ the things I hide,

Chorus

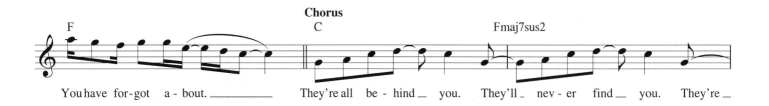

You have for-got a-bout. ___ They're all be-hind ___ you. They'll nev-er find ___ you. They're

_____ on the o - cean floor. _____ Your sins are for - got - ten. They're _____

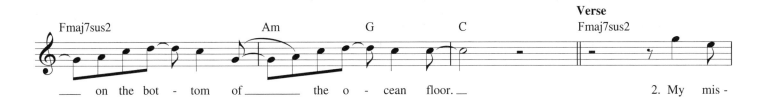

_____ on the bot - tom of _____ the o - cean floor. _____ 2. My mis -

Verse

deeds, all my grief, _____ all the things that haunt _ me now, _____

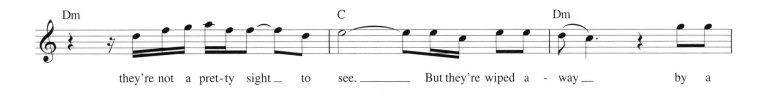

they're not a pret-ty sight _ to see. _____ But they're wiped a - way _____ by a

Chorus

might - y, might - y wave, a might - y, might - y wave, yeah. _ They're all be - hind _ you. They'll _

_____ nev - er find _ you. They're _ on the o - cean floor. _____ Your sins are for - got - ten. They're _

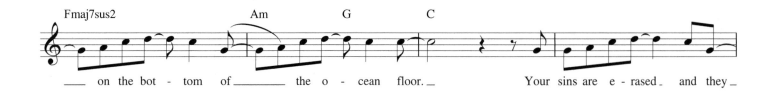

on the bot - tom of the o - cean floor. _ Your sins are e - rased_ and they_

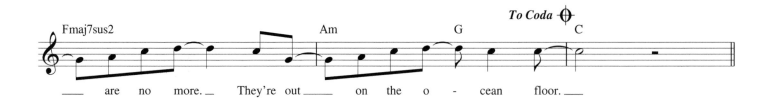

_ are no more._ They're out _ on the o - cean floor. _

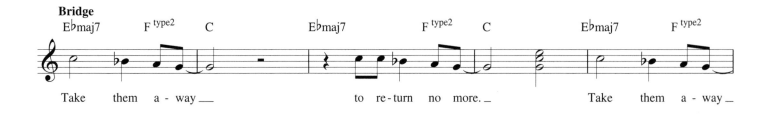

Bridge

Take them a - way _ to re - turn no more. _ Take them a - way _

D.S. al Coda

_ to the o - cean floor, to the o - cean floor.

Coda

_ Your sins are for - got - ten. They're_ on the bot - tom of _

_ the o - cean floor. _ Your sins are e - rased _ and they_

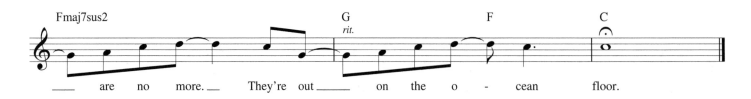

_ are no more. _ They're out _ on the o - cean floor.

Open Skies

Words and Music by David Crowder

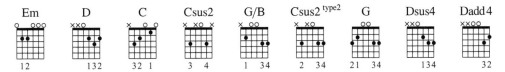

*Tune down 1/2 step:
(low to high) E♭–A♭–D♭–G♭–B♭–E♭

Strum Pattern: 6
Pick Pattern: 5

Intro
Moderately

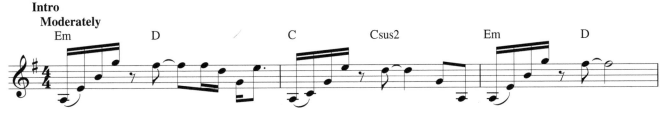

*Optional: To match recording, tune down 1/2 step.

%: Verse

1., 2. Praise Him un-der o-pen skies; ev'ry-thing breath-ing prais-ing God

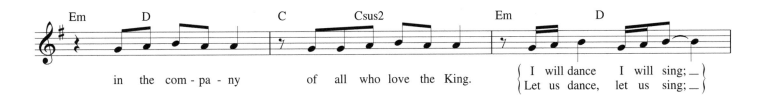

in the com-pa-ny   of all who love the King.

{ I will dance   I will sing; __ }
{ Let us dance,   let us sing; __ }

To Coda ⊕

it could be heav-en-ly.   Turn the mu-sic loud,   lift my voice and shout.   From where I am,

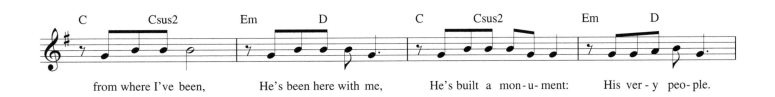

from where I've been,   He's been here with me,   He's built a mon-u-ment: His ver-y peo-ple.

lift up your head and sing to the One who gave His {love, — / Son. —} This is our of - fer - ing.

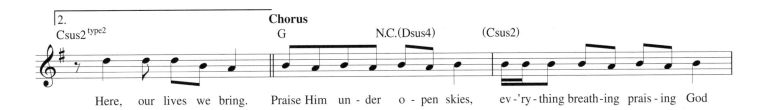

Here, our lives we bring. Praise Him un - der o - pen skies, ev -'ry-thing breath-ing prais -ing God

in the com - pan - y of all who love the King. Praise Him un - der o - pen skies;

ev -'ry-thing breath-ing prais -ing God in the com - pan - y of all who love the King.

From where - ev - er you are, where-ev - er you've been, He's been there. — So let His peo - ple

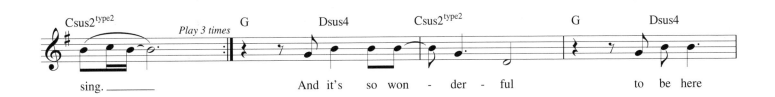

sing. _____ And it's so won - der - ful to be here

now. Wher - ev - er you are, wher - ev - er you've been, __ He's been there. —

Oh Lord, You're Beautiful

Words and Music by Keith Green

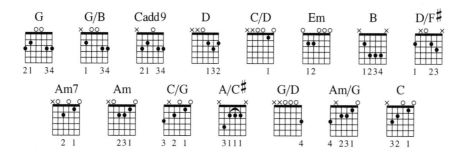

Strum Pattern: 2
Pick Pattern: 2

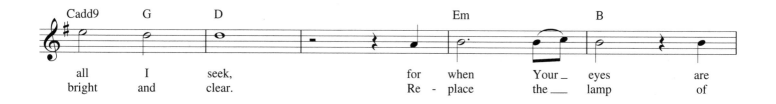

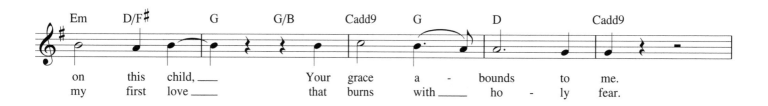

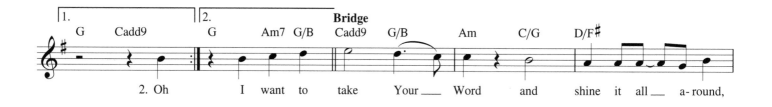

do - ing well, help me __ to nev - er seek a crown, for my re-ward is giv-ing

D.S. al Coda
(take 2nd ending)

To Coda

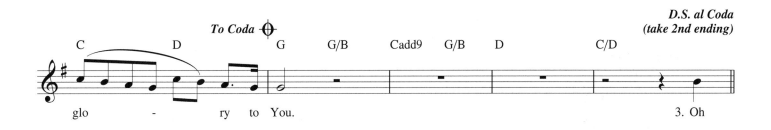

glo - ry to You.

3. Oh

 Coda

You.

Oh

Outro-Verse

Lord, You're beau - ti - ful. Your face is

all I seek, for when Your __ eyes are

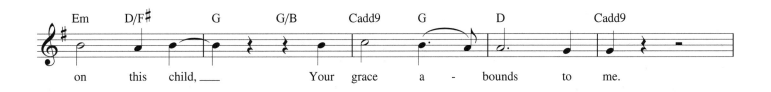

on this child, __ Your grace a - bounds to me.

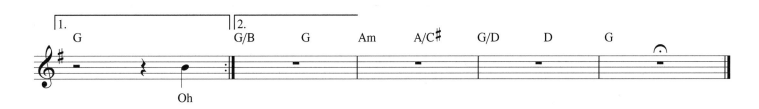

Oh

Open the Eyes of My Heart

Words and Music by Paul Baloche

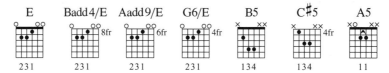

*Capo II

Strum Pattern: 4, 5
Pick Pattern: 3, 4

Verse

1., 2. O-pen the eyes — of my heart, — Lord. — O-pen the eyes — of my heart. — I want to

*Optional: To match recording, place capo at 2nd fret.

see You. — I want to see You. — O-pen the eyes — of my heart, —

— Lord. — O-pen the eyes — of my heart. — I want to see You. — I want to

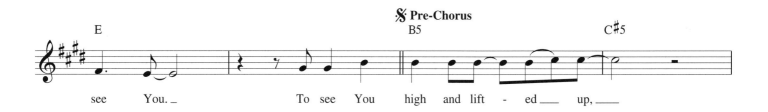

see You. — To see You high and lift - ed — up,

shin-ing in the light of Your glo - ry. — Pour out Your pow-er and love, — as we sing,

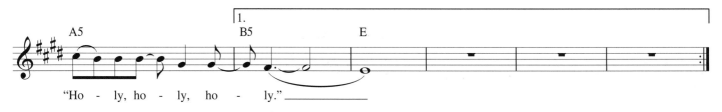

"Ho - ly, ho - ly, ho - ly." —

127

People Need the Lord

Words and Music by Phill McHugh and Greg Nelson

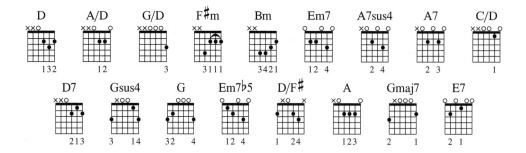

Strum Pattern: 3
Pick Pattern: 3

Verse
Moderately

1. Ev - 'ry day they pass me by, ___	I can see it
2. We are called to take His light ___	to a world where

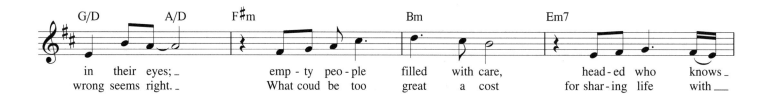

in their eyes; _	emp - ty peo - ple filled with care,	head - ed who knows _
wrong seems right. _	What coud be too great a cost	for shar - ing life with __

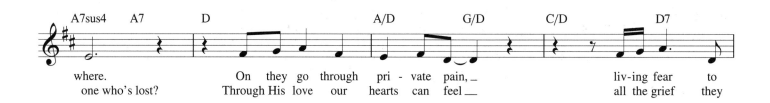

where.	On they go through pri - vate pain, _	liv - ing fear to
one who's lost?	Through His love our hearts can feel __	all the grief they

fear.	Laugh - ter hides the si - lent cries; _	on - ly Je - sus
bear.	They must hear the words of life; __	on - ly we can

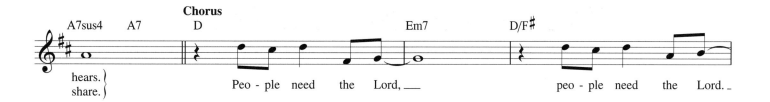

Chorus

hears.
share.

Peo - ple need the Lord, ___ peo - ple need the Lord. ___

___ At the end of bro - ken dreams, ___ He's the o - pen

door. Peo - ple need the Lord, ___ peo - ple need the Lord. ___

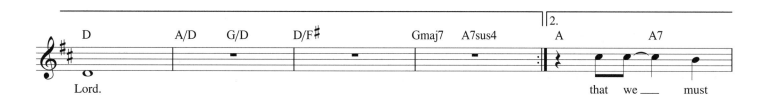

1.

___ When will ___ we re - al - ize ___ peo-ple need the

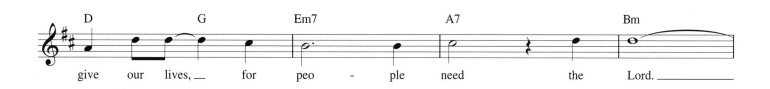

2.

Lord. that we ___ must

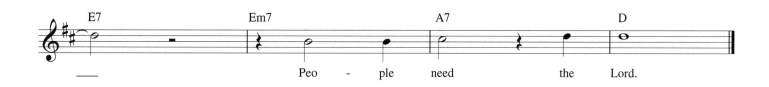

give our lives, ___ for peo - ple need the Lord. _____

E7   Em7   A7   D

___ Peo - ple need the Lord.

Praise You in This Storm

Words and Music by Mark Hall and Bernie Herms

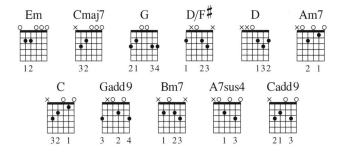

*Tune down 1/2 step:
(low to high) E♭–A♭–D♭–G♭–B♭–E♭

Strum Pattern: 3
Pick Pattern: 1

Verse
Moderately slow

1. I was sure _ by now, God, You would have _ reached down and wiped our tears _

2. *See additional lyrics*

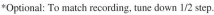

*Optional: To match recording, tune down 1/2 step.

____ a - way, stepped in and saved the day. _ But once a - gain, I say, _ "A -

Pre-Chorus

men," and it's still rain - ing. But as the thun - der rolls, I

bare - ly hear _ You whis - per through _ the rain, "I'm with ____ you." And

as Your mer - cy falls, I raise my hands _ and praise the God _ who gives and takes a - way. _

Chorus

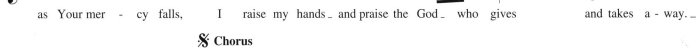

And I'll praise You in ____ this storm, and I will lift _ my

hands, _ for You are who _ You are, no mat - ter where _ I am. And ev - 'ry tear _ I've

Additional Lyrics

2. I remember when I stumbled in the wind.
   You heard my cry to You, and raised me up again.
   But my strength is almost gone.
   How can I carry on if I can't find You?

Pray

Words and Music by Rebecca St. James, Michael Quinlan and Tedd Tjornhom

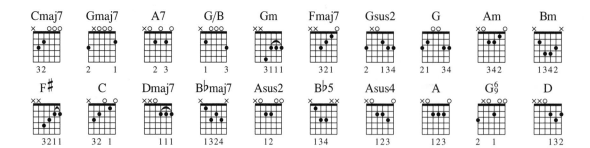

Strum Pattern: 1
Pick Pattern: 5

Intro
Moderately

1. Je - sus, I am bro - ken now. Be - fore

You I fall. I lay me down. All I want is You, my

all. I cry out from the ash - es, burned with sin and shame. I ask

You, Lord, to make me whole a - gain. For You say if I will come and will

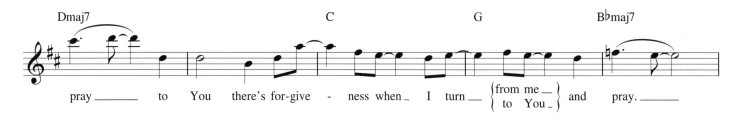

pray to You there's for-give - ness when I turn { from me / to You } and pray.

Testify to Love

Words and Music by Paul Field, Henk Pool, Ralph Van Manen and Robert Riekerk

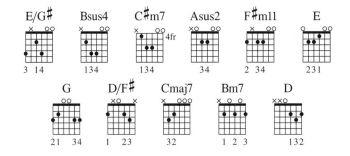

*Tune down 1/2 step:
(low to high) E♭–A♭–D♭–G♭–B♭–E♭

Strum Pattern: 1
Pick Pattern: 1

Verse
Moderately

1. All the col-ors of the rain-bow, ___ all the voic-es of ___ the wind,
2. *See additional lyrics*

*Optional: To match recording, tune down 1/2 step.

ev-'ry dream that reach - es out, ___ that reach-es out ___ to find where love ___ be-

gins, ___ ev-'ry word of ev - 'ry sto-ry, ev-'ry star in ev-'ry

135

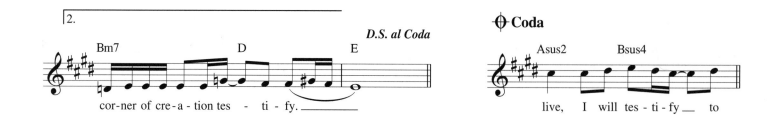

cor-ner of cre-a-tion tes - ti - fy. _____

live, I will tes-ti-fy _____ to

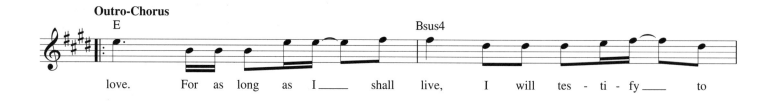

love. For as long as I _____ shall live, I will tes - ti - fy _____ to

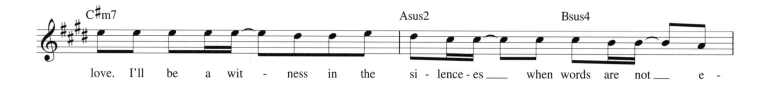

love. I'll be a wit - ness in the si - lence-es _____ when words are not _____ e -

nough. _____ With ev - 'ry breath _ I take, I will give thanks to God _ a -

bove. _____ For as long as I _____ shall live, I will tes - ti - fy _____ to

Additional Lyrics

2. From the mountains to the valleys,
From the rivers to the sea,
Every hand that reaches out,
Every hand that reaches out to offer peace,
Every simple act of mercy,
Every step to kingdom come,
All the hope in every heart
Will speak what love has done.

Shut Me Out

Words and Music by Jon Micah Sumrall and Ethan Luck

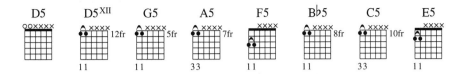

*Drop D tuning, down 1/2 step:
(low to high) D♭–A♭–D♭–G♭–B♭–E♭

Strum Pattern: 1

Intro
Moderately

*Notation and chord frames reflect drop D tuning.
Tuning down 1/2 step is optional to match recording.

Verse
Half-time feel

1. Tell me some-thing I don't al-read-y know. ___ I

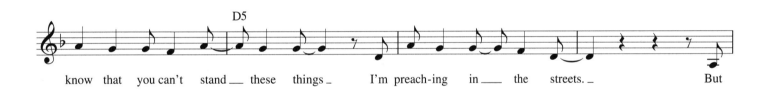

know that you can't stand ___ these things ___ I'm preach-ing in ___ the streets. ___ But

how can I con-tain ___ the truth I hold in-side ___ with

all the hurt-ing peo-ple that I see? ___ So I ___ don't ___ mind ___

put-ting up ___ with ___ you ___ and all the things ___ you say. _____ I'm

C5   D5   D5 XII   G5 A5 F5

not a - bout _ to stop ___ or e - ven change _ my _ ways. _ There's

D5   D5 XII   G5   A5 F5   D5   D5 XII   G5   A5 F5   Bb5   C5

noth - ing ___ you ___ can say ____ that will take ___ me a - way _ from this life. _

D5   D5 XII   G5 A5 F5   D5   D5 XII   G5 A5 F5   D5   D5 XII   G5 A5 F5

To Coda ⊕

_ There's noth - ing ___ you ___ can ___ do ____ to shut me up _

Bb5   C5   D5   C5

_ when I'm speak - in' the truth. _ 2. You may not like ___ all I have to say, _

G5   D5

_ but you can't prove _ that ev - 'ry - thing _ is filled with emp - ty words. _

                     C5   G5

_ I know my life ____ and in - side how I've changed, _ a

D.S. al Coda

              D5   E5   F5

tes - ti - mo - ny to ____ the truth _ I speak. _ So I ___ don't _ mind _

⊕ **Coda**

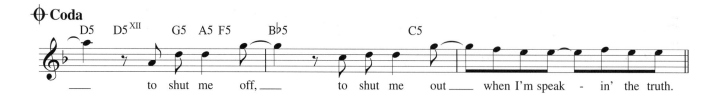

D5   D5 XII   G5   A5 F5   Bb5   C5

_ to shut me off, ___ to shut me out ___ when I'm speak - in' the truth.

Interlude

Chorus
w/ Intro rhy.

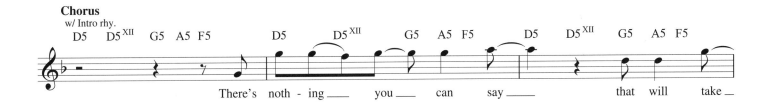

There's noth - ing ___ you ___ can say ___ that will take ___

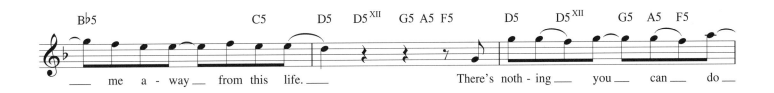

___ me a - way ___ from this life. ___ There's noth - ing ___ you ___ can ___ do ___

___ to shut me up ___ when I'm speak - in' the truth. ___ There's

noth - ing ___ you ___ can say ___ that will take ___ me a - way ___ from this life. ___

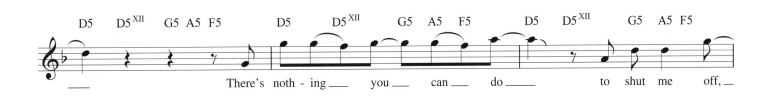

___ There's noth - ing ___ you ___ can ___ do ___ to shut me off, ___

___ to shut me out ___ when I'm speak - in' the truth. ___

Run to You

Words and Music by Twila Paris

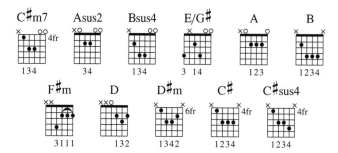

Strum Pattern: 3, 4
Pick Pattern: 3, 4

1. Fast - er now _ than ev - er, __
2. *See additional lyrics*

I run _ to You. Now I know _ You bet - ter, __ I run _ to You.

I am a lit - tle old - er now, You know _ it's true. May - be a lit - tle

wis - er, too, I run _ to You. And I ___ can see, (I ___ can see.)

deep - er than I did be - fore. I do _ be - lieve, (I ___ be - lieve.) Nev - er have I been so

sure that I need _ You ev - 'ry {min - ute, ev - 'ry day. ___}
{foot - step, all _ the way. ___}

That I need _ {You more _ than I ___ could ev - er say. ___}
{You so _ much more _ than I can say. ___}

Additional Lyrics

2. Even on the sad days, I run to You.
Even on the good days, too, I run to You.
Even before all else fails, You know it's true.
You are the wind in my sails, I run to You.

Shine on Us

Words and Music by Michael W. Smith and Debbie Smith

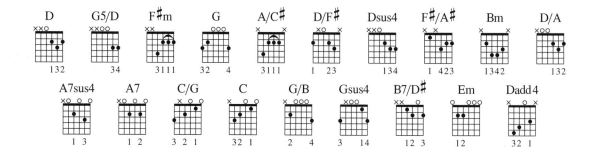

Strum Pattern: 2
Pick Pattern: 2, 4

Verse
Moderately

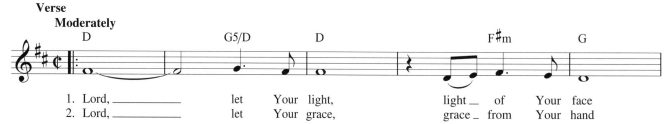

1. Lord, _____ let Your light, light _ of Your face
2. Lord, _____ let Your grace, grace _ from Your hand

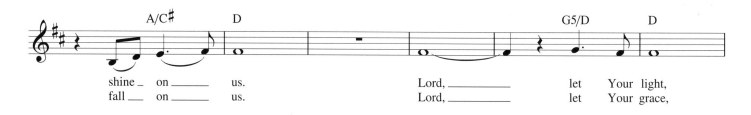

shine _ on _____ us.   Lord, _____ let Your light,
fall _ on _____ us.   Lord, _____ let Your grace,

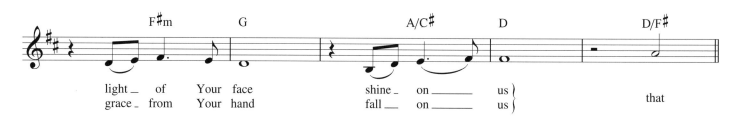

light _ of Your face   shine _ on _____ us }
grace _ from Your hand   fall _ on _____ us }   that

Chorus

we _____ may be saved,   that we _____ may have life

to find our way _____ in the dark - est night. _____   { Let Your light _
{ Let Your grace _

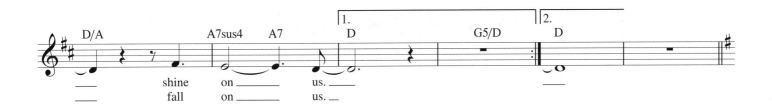

shine on ___ us. ___
fall on ___ us. ___

Verse

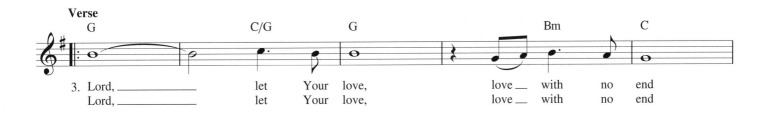

3. Lord, _____ let Your love, love ___ with no end
Lord, _____ let Your love, love ___ with no end

come _ o - ver us. _____
come _ o - ver us _____ that we _____ may be saved,

Chorus

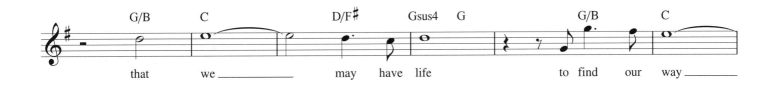

that we _____ may have life to find our way _____

A tempo

___ in the dark - est night. _____ Let Your love ___ come o - ver us.

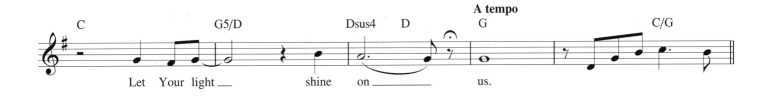

A tempo

Let Your light ___ shine on _____ us.

Outro

rit.

Sing Your Praise to the Lord

Words and Music by Richard Mullins

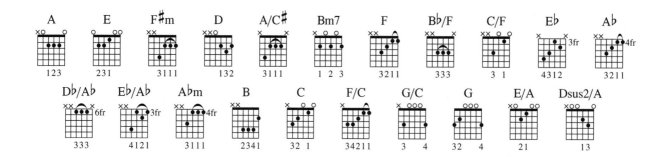

Strum Pattern: 6, 2
Pick Pattern: 4

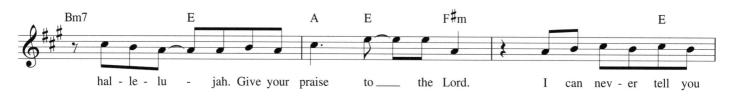

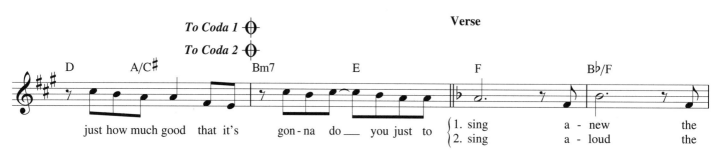

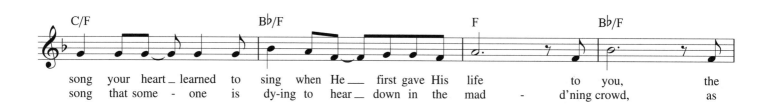

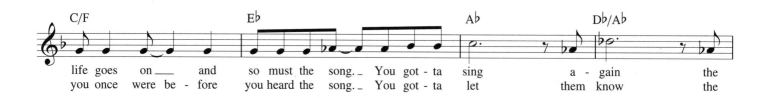

song born ___ in your soul when you ___ first gave your heart to Him.
truth is a - live to shine up-on the way so may - be they can go,

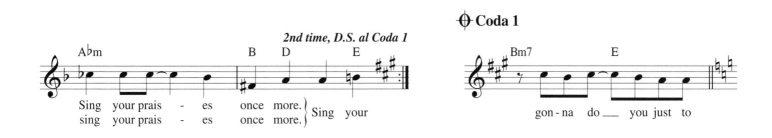

2nd time, D.S. al Coda 1

Sing your prais - es once more.
sing your prais - es once more. } Sing your

$\oplus$ **Coda 1**

gon - na do ___ you just to

Bridge

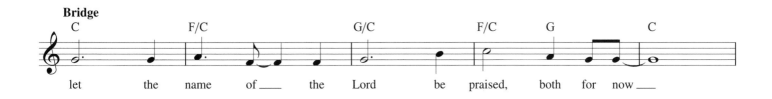

let the name of ___ the Lord be praised, both for now ___

D.S. al Coda 2

and ev - er - more. ___ Praise Him all ___ you ser - vants. Give your

$\oplus$ **Coda 2**

Outro

gon - na do ___ you just to sing, sing, ___ sing. ___ Sing, sing, ___ sing. ___

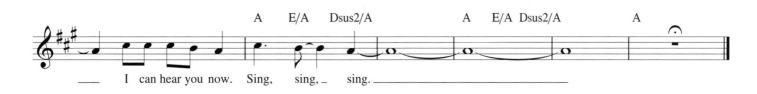

___ I can hear you now. Sing, sing, ___ sing. ___

So Long Self

Words and Music by Bart Millard, Barry Graul, Jim Bryson,
Nathan Cochran, Mike Scheuchzer and Robby Shaffer

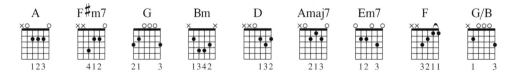

*Tune down 1/2 step:
(low to high) E♭–A♭–D♭–G♭–B♭–E♭

Strum Pattern: 1
Pick Pattern: 3

Verse
Moderately fast

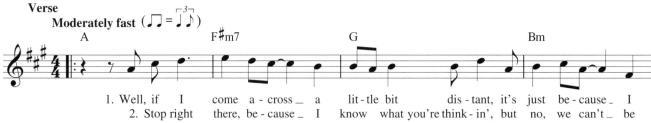

1. Well, if I come a-cross__ a lit-tle bit dis-tant, it's just be-cause__ I
2. Stop right there, be-cause__ I know what you're think-in', but no, we can't__ be

*Optional: To match recording, tune down 1/2 step.

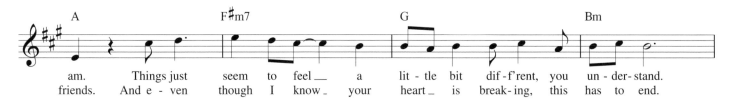

am. Things just seem to feel__ a lit-tle bit dif-f'rent, you un-der-stand.
friends. And e-ven though I know__ your heart__ is break-ing, this has to end.

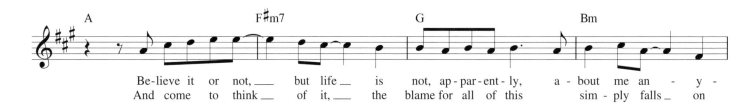

Be-lieve it or not,__ but life__ is not, ap-par-ent-ly, a-bout me an-y-
And come to think__ of it,__ the blame for all of this sim-ply falls__ on

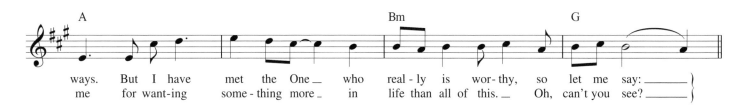

ways. But I have met the One__ who real-ly is wor-thy, so let me say:__
me for want-ing some-thing more__ in life than all of this.__ Oh, can't you see?__

Chorus

So long self;__ well, it's been fun, but I__ have found__ some-bod-y else. So long self;__

__ there's just no room for two,__ so you__ are gon-na have to move. So long self;__

don't take this wrong, but you _ are wrong _ for me. Fare - well, oh well, good - bye, don't cry. _

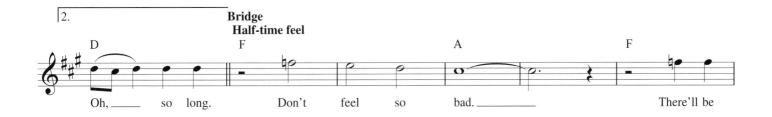

To Coda ⊕ 1.

Oh, _ so long self.

2.

Bridge
Half-time feel

Oh, _ so long. Don't feel so bad. _ There'll be

bet - ter _ days. _ Don't go a - way _ mad, but

Interlude
End half-time feel

by all means, just go a - way. _ Go a - way. _

D.S. al Coda

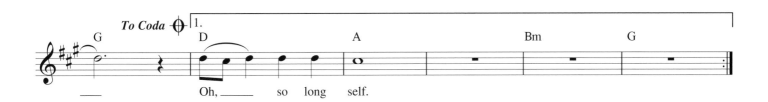

⊕ **Coda**

Outro

Repeat and fade

Oh, _ so long self. _ Fare - well, good - bye. Oh, _ so long.

Sometimes He Calms the Storm

Words and Music by Kevin Stokes and Tony Wood

Strum Pattern: 6
Pick Pattern: 4

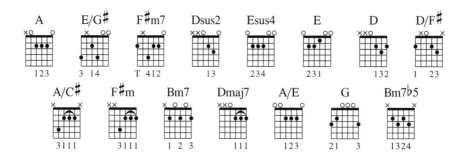

1. All who sail __ the sea __ of faith __ find out be-fore __ too long
2. *See additional lyrics*

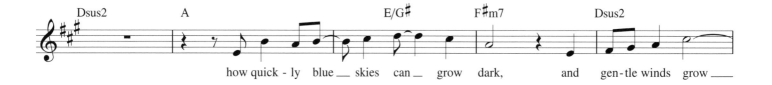

how quick - ly blue __ skies can __ grow dark, and gen-tle winds grow __

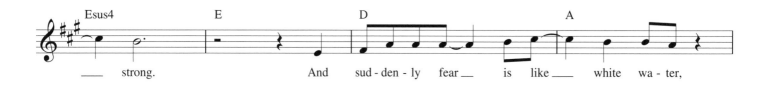

__ strong. And sud-den-ly fear __ is like __ white wa - ter,

pound - ing on __ the soul ____ and still __ we sail __ on, know-ing that our

Lord is in __ con - trol. __ Some-times He calms __ the storm __ with a

whis - pered, "Peace, _ be still." He can set - tle an - y sea, _____ but it does-n't mean _

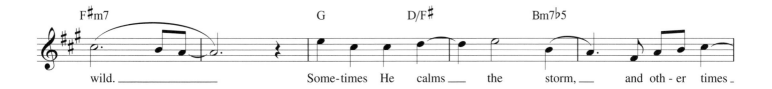

_____ He will. Some-times He holds _____ us close _____ and lets the wind and waves _ go

wild. _____ Some-times He calms _____ the storm, _____ and oth - er times _

To Coda ⊕ |1.

_____ He calms _ His child.

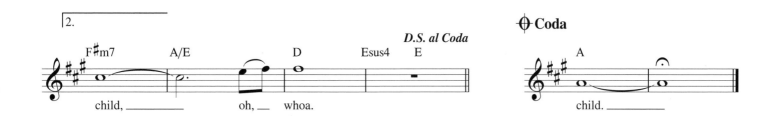

|2.

D.S. al Coda

⊕ **Coda**

child, _____ oh, _ whoa. child. _____

Additional Lyrics

2. He has a reason for each trial
That we pass through in life,
And though we're shaken,
We cannot be pulled apart from Christ.
No matter how the driving rain beats down
On those who hold to faith,
A heart of trust will always
Be a quiet, peaceful place.

Song of Love

Words and Music by Rebecca St. James, Matt Bronleewe and Jeremy Ash

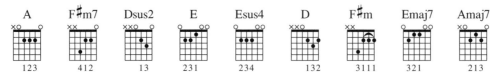

*Capo 1

Strum Pattern: 6
Pick Pattern: 4

Verse
Moderately

1. Je - sus, ___ King of my heart. ___ Fa - ther, ___ my peace and my light. ___

*Optional: To match recording, place capo at 1st fret.

Spir - it, ___ the joy of my soul ___ You are. ___ 2. Je - sus, ___ to 3. *See additional lyrics*

You none com - pare. ___ Fa - ther, ___ I rest in Your care. ___ Spir - it, ___ the

hope for my heart _ You are. ___ The heav - ens ___ de - clare You are God, _ and the

moun - tains ___ re - joice. ___ The o - ceans ___ cry, "Al - le - lu - ia," ___ as we

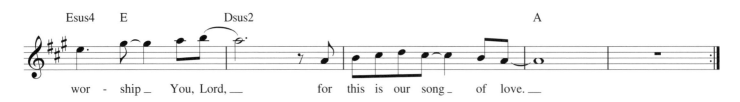

wor - ship ___ You, Lord, ___ for this is our song ___ of love.

Bridge

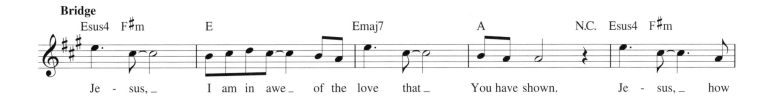

Je - sus, _ I am in awe _ of the love that _ You have shown. Je - sus, _ how

pre - cious You are ___ to me, ___ to me. ___ The heav - ens ___ de -

Chorus

clare You are God, ___ and the moun - tains ___ re - joice. ___ The o - ceans ___ cry,

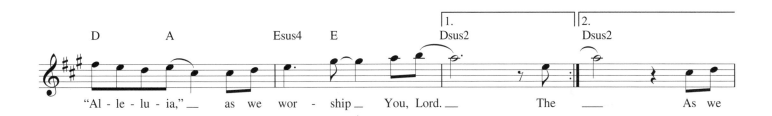

"Al - le - lu - ia," ___ as we wor - ship _ You, Lord. ___ The ___ As we

Outro

wor - ship _ You, Lord, ___ for this is our song _ of love. ___ Our song of

*Tie 1st time only.

Repeat and fade

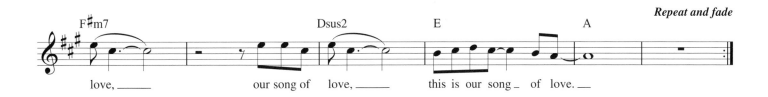

love, ___ our song of love, ___ this is our song _ of love. ___

Additional Lyrics

3. Jesus, You saved my soul.
I'll thank You forevermore.
Jesus, the love of my life You are.

Speechless

Words and Music by Steven Curtis Chapman and Geoff Moore

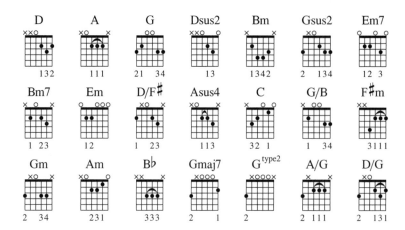

Strum Pattern: 2
Pick Pattern: 3

Intro
Moderately

Verse

1. Words fall __ like drops of rain; __ my lips are __ like clouds.
2. *See additional lyrics*

I say __ so man-y things __ try-ing __ to fig-ure You out. _____

But as mer - cy o-pens my eyes __ and my words __ are stol-en a-

way, _____ with this breath-tak - ing view of __ Your grace. And I am

Chorus

speech - less. __ I'm a - ston - ished and a - mazed. I am si - lenced __ by Your

won - drous __ grace. __ You have saved me, __ You have raised me __ from the grave.

And I am speech - less __ in Your pres - ence __ now. __ I'm a -

stound - ed __ as I con - sid - er __ how __ You have shown us __ a love that

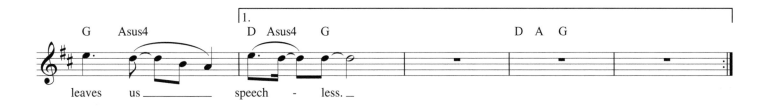

leaves us __ speech - less. __

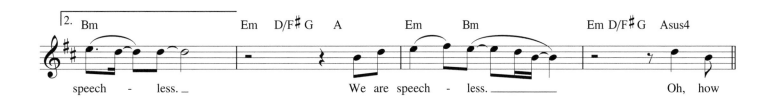

speech - less. __ We are speech - less. __ Oh, how

Bridge

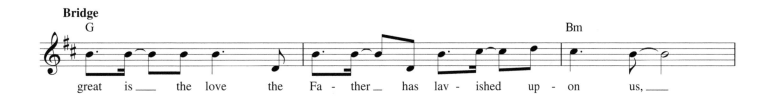

great is __ the love the Fa - ther __ has lav - ished up - on us, __

153

that we should _ be called the sons and _ the daugh-ters _ of

God. _____

Outro

We stand _ in awe of _ Your grace. We stand _ in awe of _ Your mer - cy. _

We stand _ in awe of _ Your love. We are _ speech - less. _

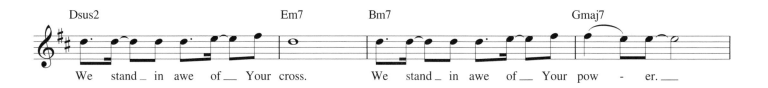

We stand _ in awe of _ Your cross. We stand _ in awe of _ Your pow - er. _

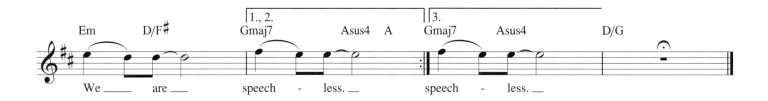

We _ are _ speech - less. _ speech - less. _

Additional Lyrics

2. So what kind of love could this be,
   That would trade heaven's throne for a cross?
   And to think You still celebrate
   Over finding just one who was lost.
   And to know You rejoice over us,
   The God of the whole universe,
   It's a story that's too great for words.

Take You Back

Words and Music by Jeremy Camp

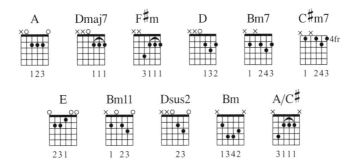

Strum Pattern: 1
Pick Pattern: 3

Intro
Moderately

Verse

1. The rea - son why I stand, the an - swer lies __ in
2. *See additional lyrics*

You. You hung to make __ me strong, though my praise __ was

few. When I fall, ___ I bring __ Your name __ down. But I have found __ in

You a heart ___ that bleeds __ for - give - ness, __ re - plac - ing all ___ these

thoughts of pain - ful mem - o - ries. ___ But I

Outro-Chorus

Additional Lyrics

2. You satisfy this cry of what I'm lookin' for,
And I'll take all I can and lay it down before
The throne of endless grace, now, that radiates what's true.
I'm in the only place that erases all these faults
That have overtaken me.
But I know that Your response will always be:

Strong Tower

Words and Music by Marc Byrd, Mark Lee, Jon Micah Sumrall and Aaron Sprinkle

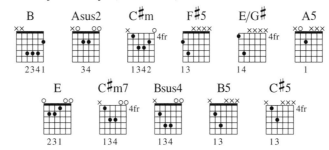

Strum Pattern: 3
Pick Pattern: 1

Verse
Moderately

1. When I wan-der through the des-ert and I'm long-ing for __ my
2. *See additional lyrics*

home, all my dreams have gone __ a-stray. When I'm strand-ed in __ the

val-ley and I'm tired and all __ a-lone, it seems like I've lost __ my way.

§ Pre-Chorus

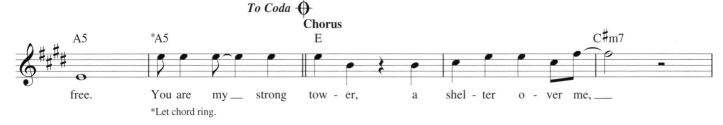

1., 3. I go
2. Now I'm } run-ning to __ Your moun-tain, where Your mer-cy sets __ me

To Coda ⊕
Chorus

free.   You are my __ strong tow-er, a shel-ter o-ver me, __

*Let chord ring.

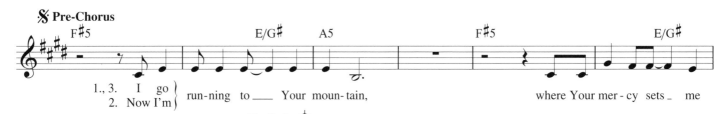

beau-ti-ful __ and might-y, ev-er-last-ing King. You are my __ strong

tow-er, a for-tress when I'm weak. __ Your name is true and ho-ly,

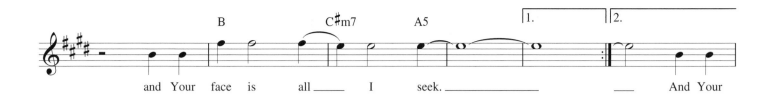

B   C#m7   A5

and Your face is all ___ I seek. _____ ___ And Your

B   C#m7   A5   B   C#m7   A5

face is all ___ I seek. ___ Yeah, _ Your face is all ___ I seek. _

D.S. al Coda   ⊕ **Coda**

Outro-Chorus

E   C#m7

_____   tow - er, a shel - ter o - ver me, ___

Asus2   Bsus4

beau-ti - ful __ and might - y, ev - er-last - ing King. You are my _ strong

E   C#m7   Asus2

tow - er, a for - tress when I'm weak. _ Your name is true and ho - ly,

1.   Bsus4   2.   B   C#m7   A5

You are my _ strong   and Your face is all ___ I seek. _

B5   C#5   A5

_____

Additional Lyrics

2. In the middle of my darkness,
   In the midst of all my fear,
   You're my refuge and my hope.
   When the storm of life is raging,
   And the thunder's all I hear,
   You speak softly to my soul.

There Is a Redeemer

Words and Music by Melody Green

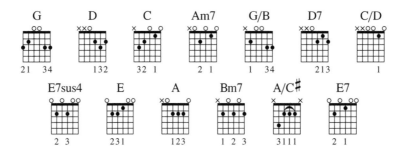

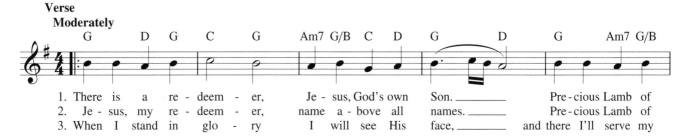

Strum Pattern: 1, 3
Pick Pattern: 3, 5

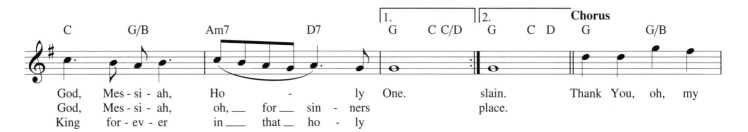

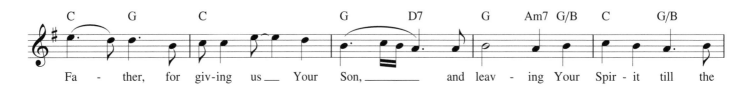

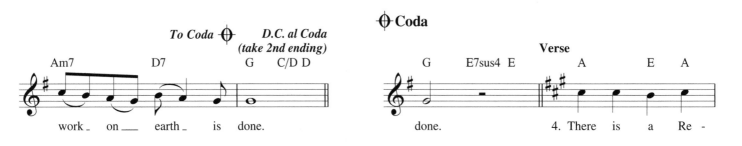

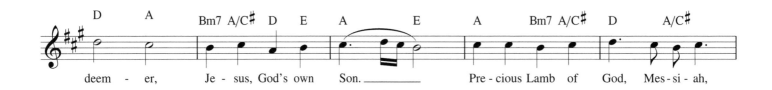

Chorus

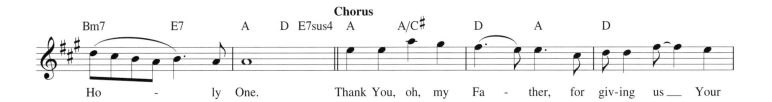

Ho - ly One. Thank You, oh, my Fa - ther, for giv-ing us __ Your

Son, _____ and leav - ing Your Spir - it till the work __ on __ earth __ is done. And

Outro

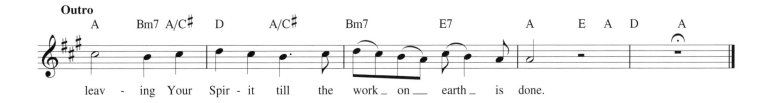

leav - ing Your Spir - it till the work __ on __ earth __ is done.

Thy Word

Words and Music by Michael W. Smith and Amy Grant

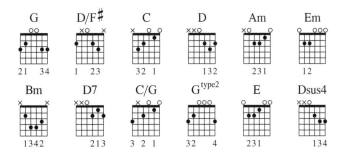

Strum Pattern: 1, 2
Pick Pattern: 2, 4

Chorus
Moderately

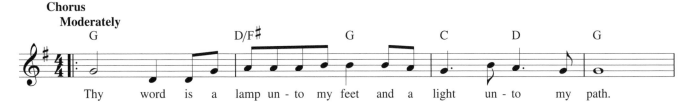

Thy word is a lamp un - to my feet and a light un - to my path.

To Coda ⊕

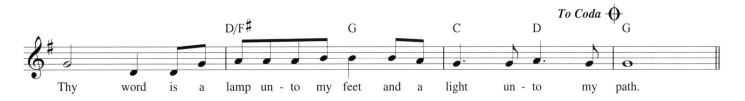

Thy word is a lamp un - to my feet and a light un - to my path.

Verse

1. When I am a - fraid, think I've lost my way, still, You're there right be - side _____ me. And
2. *See additional lyrics*

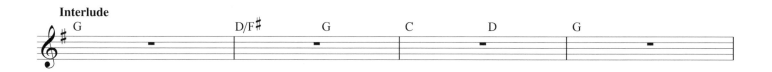

noth-ing will I fear as ___ long as You are near. Please be near me to the end. _____

Interlude

Bridge

D.C. al Coda

Noth-ing will I fear as ___ long as You are near. Please be near me to the end. _____

Coda

path, and a light un - to my path. You're the light un - to my path. _____

Additional Lyrics

2. I will not forget Your love for me and yet,
My heart forever is wandering.
Jesus, be my guide, and hold me to Your side
And I will love You to the end.

This Is Your Time

Words and Music by Michael W. Smith and Wes King

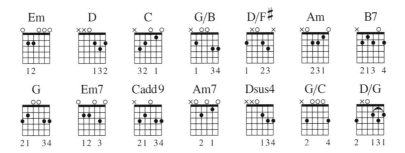

*Capo III

Strum Pattern: 7, 8
Pick Pattern: 7, 9

Verse
Moderately

1. It was a test __ we could all __ hope to pass, __ but none of us would __
2. *See additional lyrics*

*Optional: To match recording, place capo at 3rd fret.

__ want __ to take. __ Faced with the choice __ to de - ny __

__ God and live, __ for her there was one __ choice to make. __

Chorus

This was her time, __ this was her dance. __ She lived ev - 'ry mo - ment, left

noth - ing __ to chance. __ She swam in the sea, __ drank from the deep, __

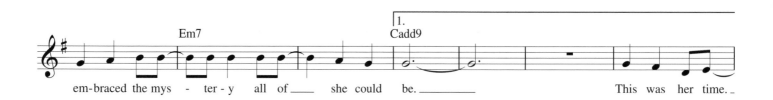
em-braced the mys - ter - y all of ___ she could be. ___ This was her time. _

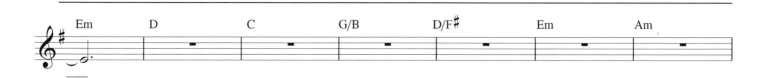

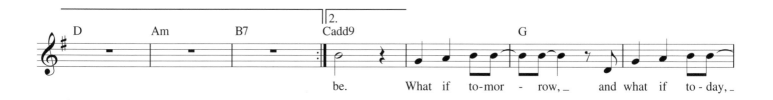
be. What if to-mor - row, _ and what if to - day, _

faced with the ques - tion, oh, what would you say? ___

Interlude

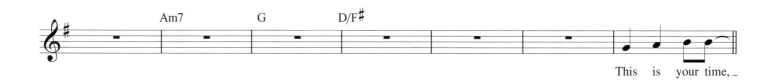
This is your time, _

Chorus

___ this is your dance. _ Live ev - 'ry mo - ment, leave noth-ing _ to chance.

Swim in the sea, ___ drink of the deep, _ fall on the mer - cy and hear _

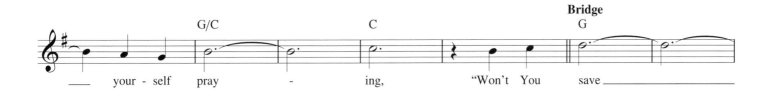

your - self   pray   -   ing,   "Won't   You   save _____

_____   me?" _____   "Won't   You   save _____

_____   me?" _____   This   is   your   time, _

Outro-Chorus

_____   this   is   your   dance. _   Live   ev - 'ry   mo - ment, leave   no - thing _   to

chance.   Swim   in   the   sea, _____   drink   of   the   deep, _____   em - brace   the mys -

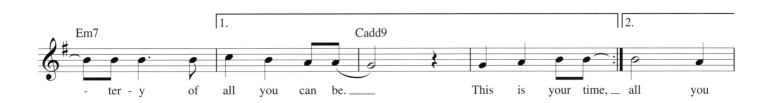

- ter - y   of   all   you   can   be. _____   This   is   your   time, _   all   you

can   be. _____   This   is   your   time. _____

Additional Lyrics

2. Though you are mourning and grieving your loss,
   Death died a long time ago.
   Swallowed in life, so her life carries on,
   Still, it's so hard to let go.

This Love

Words and Music by Margaret Becker, Charlie Peacock and Kip Summers

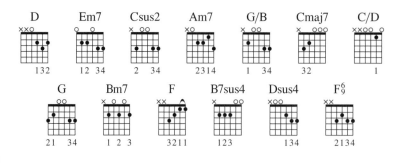

Strum Pattern: 4
Pick Pattern: 6

Verse
Moderately

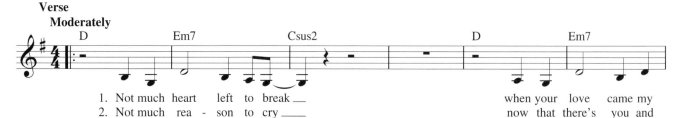

1. Not much heart left to break ___ when your love came my
2. Not much rea - son to cry ___ now that there's you and

way.
I.
I wrapped my - self in walls of steel ___
I wrapped my dreams ___ up in you ___

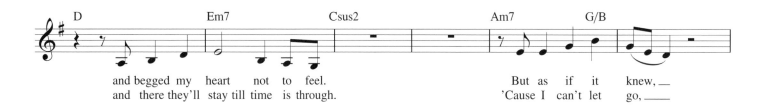

and begged my heart not to feel.
and there they'll stay till time is through.
But as if it knew, ___
'Cause I can't let go, ___

it ran straight to You.
no, I won't break free
Jumped right in - to Your arms; ___ there was noth-ing I ___ could do. ___
of this lov-ing hold ___ that You have o - ver me. ___

Chorus

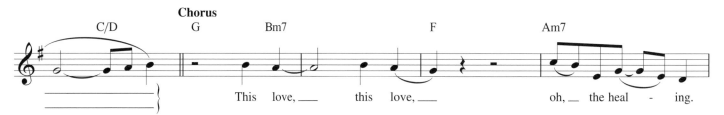

This love, ___ this love, ___ oh, ___ the heal - ing.

This love, ___ this love. ___ Tell me, tell ___ me. Where would I go, ___

what would I do ____ with - out ____ Your love? ____

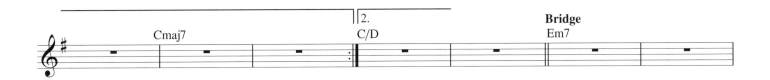

Where would I go? How could I live? ____ What would I

do? Tell me, tell me. Where would I go? ____ This love, __

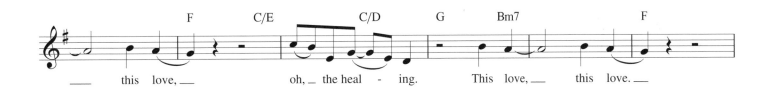
____ this love, ____ oh, __ the heal - ing. This love, ____ this love. ____

Tell me, tell __ me. Where would I go, ____ what would I do ____ with -

out ____ Your love? ____ Tell me, __ tell me, yeah.

To Know You

Words and Music by Nichole Nordeman and Mark Hammond

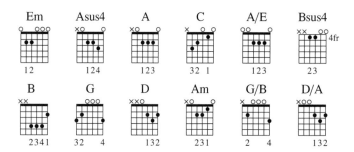

*Capo 1

Strum Pattern: 1
Pick Pattern: 3

Intro   Verse
Moderately slow

*Optional: To match recording, place capo at 1st fret.

1. It's well past mid-night   and I'm a-wake with ques-tions that won't

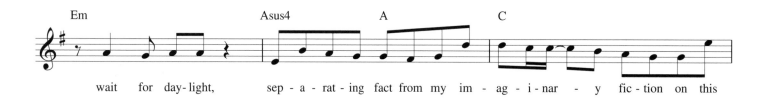

wait   for day-light,   sep-a-rat-ing fact from my im-ag-i-nar-y fic-tion on this

shelf of my __ con-vic-tion.   I need to find __ a place where You and I come face to face.

Verse

2. Thom-as need-ed   proof that You __ had real-ly ris-en un-de-feat-ed.
3. *See additional lyrics*

When he placed his fin-gers where the nails once broke Your skin, __ did his faith fi-n'lly be-gin? __ I've

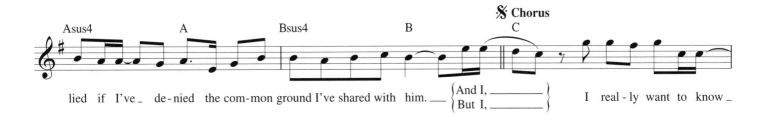

lied if I've_ de-nied the com-mon ground I've shared with him. ___ {And I, _____} {But I, _____} I real-ly want to know_

___ You. I want to make_ each day a dif-f'rent way that I___ can show You how_

___ {1., 2. I real-ly want to} {3. I'm real-ly gon-na} love_ You. _____ Be pa-tient with_ my doubt. I'm just

try'n' to fig-ure_ out Your_ will, and I real-ly want_ to know You

still. _____ real-ly want_ to know You still._ No more

camp-in' on ___ the porch_ of in - de - ci - sion, no more_

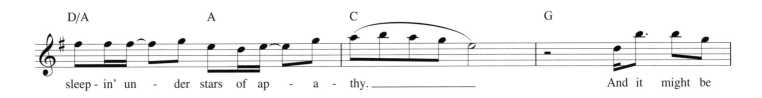

sleep-in' un - der stars of ap - a - thy. _____ And it might be

eas - i - er ___ to dream, ___ but dream-in's not for me. ___ And I ___

Coda

Outro

real - ly want ___ to know You still. ___ I want to know ___ You, ___

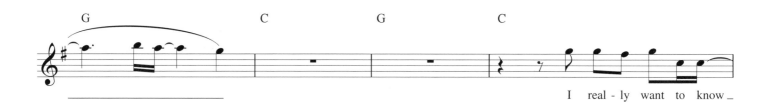

real - ly want ___ to know ___ You. Hey. ___ Hey. ___

___ I real - ly want to know ___

___ You. I real - ly want to know ___ You. ___ Ah. ___

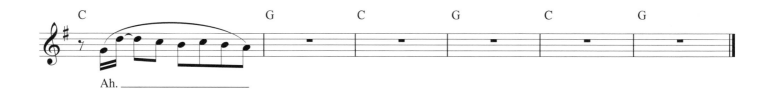

Ah. ___

Additional Lyrics

3. Nicodemus could not understand how You could truly free us.
   He struggled with the image of a grown man born again.
   We might have been good friends,
   'Cause sometimes I still question, too, how easily we come to You.

Undo Me

Words and Music by Jennifer Knapp

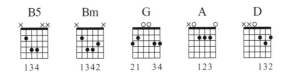

Strum Pattern: 2, 3
Pick Pattern: 3, 4

Intro
Moderately

Verse

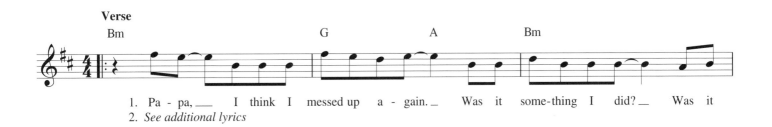

1. Pa - pa, ___ I think I messed up a - gain. ___ Was it some-thing I did? ___ Was it
2. *See additional lyrics*

some-thing I ___ said? ___ I don't mean ___ to do ___ you wrong. ___ It's just the

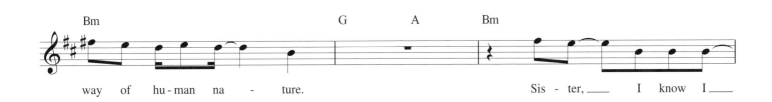

way of hu - man na - ture. Sis - ter, ___ I know I ___

___ let you down. ___ I can tell by the fact ___ you're nev - er ___ com - in' ___ 'round. ___

You don't_ have to say _ a thing. _ I can tell _ by your eyes _ ex -

𝄇 Chorus

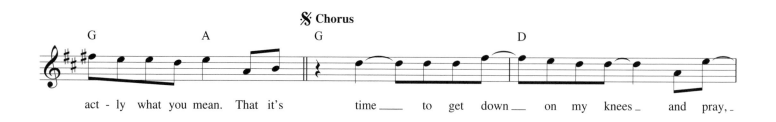

act - ly what you mean. That it's time _ to get down _ on my knees _ and pray, _

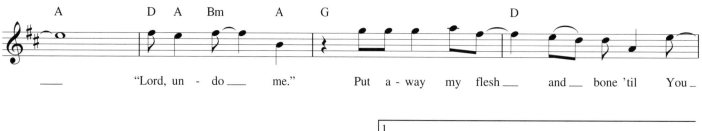

_ "Lord, un - do _ me." Put a - way my flesh _ and _ bone 'til You _

1.

To Coda ⊕

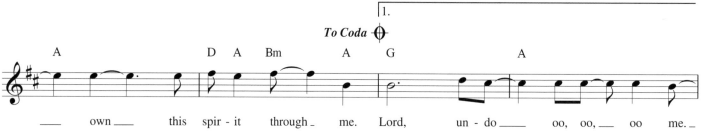

_ own _ this spir - it through _ me. Lord, un - do _ oo, oo, _ oo me. _

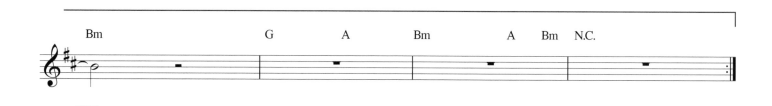

2.

Bridge

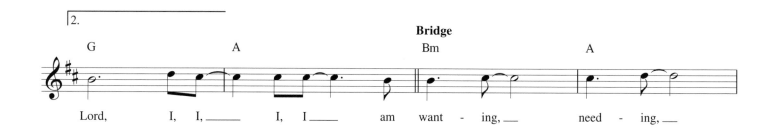

Lord, I, I, _ I, I _ am want - ing, _ need - ing, _

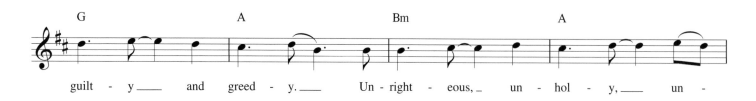

guilt - y _ and greed - y. _ Un - right - eous, _ un - hol - y, _ un -

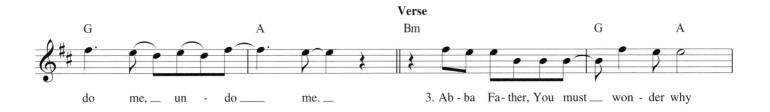

Verse

do me, __ un - do ___ me. ___   3. Ab - ba Fa - ther, You must __ won - der why

more times than Pe - ter I ___ have __ de - nied. ___ Three nails __ and a cross __

D.S. al Coda

___ to prove __ I owe ___ my life __ e - tern - 'ly to You. __ And it's time,

Coda

Outro

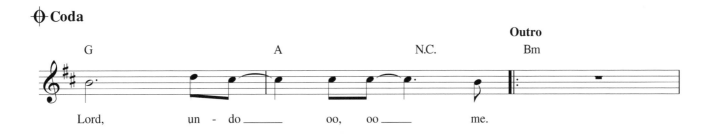

Lord, un - do ___ oo, oo ___ me.

Play 3 times

Additional Lyrics

2. Momma, I know I made you cry,
   But I never meant to hurt you,
   I never meant to lie.
   While the world shook it's head in shame,
   I let you take the blame.
   Brother, I know you labored so hard to please,
   Yeah, yeah, yeah but I cut you down
   And I left you on your knees.
   Well I know it must be...

Undivided

Words and Music by Melodie Tunney

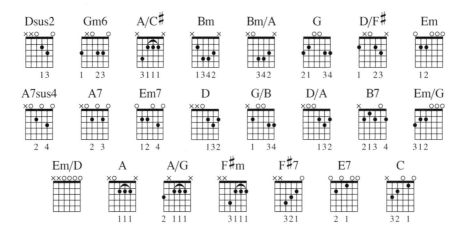

Strum Pattern: 3
Pick Pattern: 3

Lord. _____ In our hearts _____ we're un - di - vid - ed, bound by His spir - it for - ev - er -

D.S. al Coda

$\oplus$ **Coda**

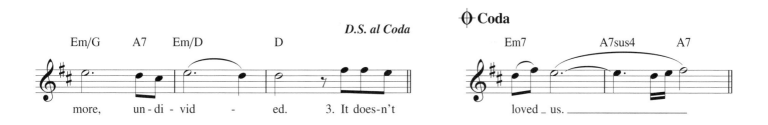

more, un - di - vid - ed. 3. It does-n't   loved _ us. _____

Bridge

He made us _____ in His im - age _____ and in His eyes we are all the same. _____

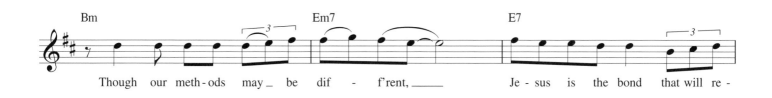

Though our meth-ods may _ be dif - f'rent, _____ Je - sus is the bond that will re -

Outro-Chorus

main. _____ In our hearts _____ we're un - di - vid - ed, wor-ship-ping one Sav-ior, one

Lord. _____ In our hearts _____ we're un - di - vid - ed, bound by His

Repeat and fade

spir - it for - ev - er - more, un - di - vid - ed. In our

Voice of Truth

Words and Music by Mark Hall and Steven Curtis Chapman

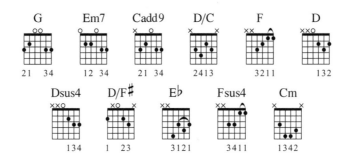

*Tune down 1 step:
(low to high) D-G-C-F-A-D

Strum Pattern: 4, 6
Pick Pattern: 4, 5

Intro
Moderately

*Optional: To match recording, tune down 1 step.

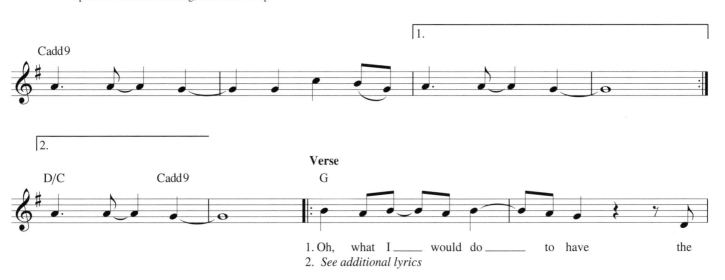

1. Oh, what I _____ would do _____ to have the
2. *See additional lyrics*

kind of faith _ it takes _____ to climb out _ of this boat I'm in, _

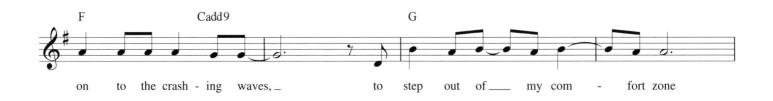

on to the crash-ing waves, _ to step out of _ my com - fort zone

in - to the realm of the ___ un-known where Je - sus is. ___ And He's

hold-ing out ___ His hand. ___ But the waves are call - ing out ___ my name ___ and they

laugh at me, ___ re - mind - ing me ___ of all ___ the times ___ I've

tried be - fore ___ and failed. ___ The waves, they keep ___ on tell - ing me

time and time ___ a - gain, _____ "Boy, _____ you'll nev - er win." "You'll

Chorus

nev - er win." But the voice of ___ truth ___

___ tells me a dif - f'rent sto - ry. The voice of ___ truth ___

___ says, "Do not be ___ a - fraid." _____ And the voice of ___ truth ___

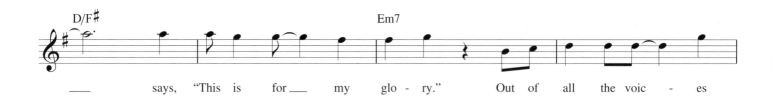

D/F#　　　　　　　　　　　　　　　　　Em7

___ says, "This is for ___ my glo - ry." Out of all the voic - es

Cadd9　　　　　　　　　　　　　　　　Em7

call - ing out ___ to ___ me, ___ I will choose ___ to lis -

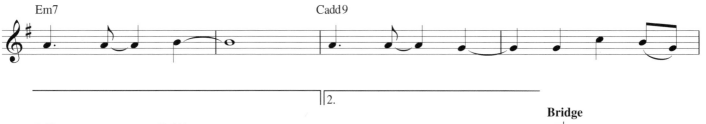

1.

Cadd9　　　　　　　　　　　　　G

- ten and ___ be - lieve ___ the voice _____ of truth.

Em7　　　　　　　　　　　　　　　Cadd9

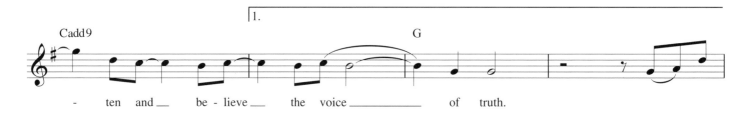

2.

　　　　　　　　　　　　　　　　　　　　　　　　Bridge
D/C　　　　　Cadd9　　　　　　　　　　　　　　　　Eb

___ the voice _ of truth. ___ But the

　　　　　　Fsus4　　　　　　　　　F　　　　　　Eb

stone was just the right ___ size to put the gi - ant on ___ the ground, ___ and the

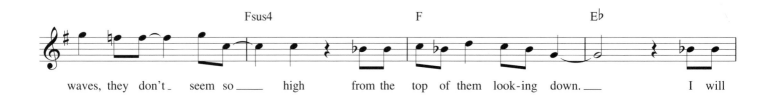

　　　　　　Fsus4　　　　　　　　　F　　　　　　Eb

waves, they don't ___ seem so _____ high from the top of them look-ing down. ___ I will

　　　　　　Fsus4　　　　　　　　　F　　　　　　Cm

soar with the wings of ea - gles when I stop and lis - ten to the sound ___

Chorus

_____ of Je - sus sing - ing o - ver me. _____ The

voice of _____ truth _____ tells me a dif - f'rent sto - ry. The

voice of _____ truth _____ says, "Do not be _____ a - fraid." _____ And the

voice of _____ truth _____ says, "This is for _____ My glo - ry." Out of

all the voic - es call - ing out _____ to _____ me, _____

I will choose _ to lis - ten and be - lieve, _____

I will choose _ to lis - ten and _____ be - lieve _____ the voice _____

Outro

_____ of truth. I will

Cadd9

lis - ten and be - lieve, I will lis - ten and be - lieve ___ the voice ___

G   Em7

___ of truth.   I will

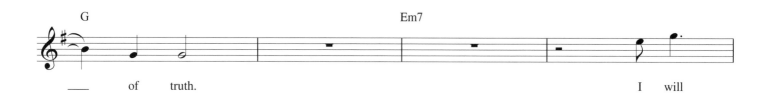

Cadd9

lis - ten and ___ be - lieve, ___ 'cause Je - sus, ___ You are ___ the voice ___

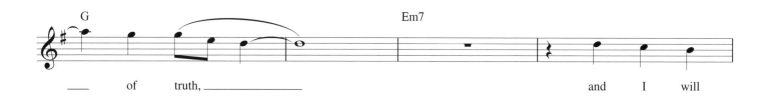

G   Em7

___ of truth, ___   and I will

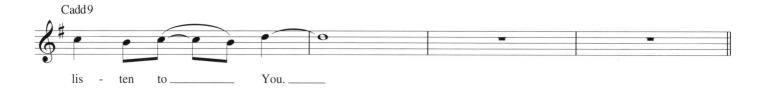

Cadd9

lis - ten to ___ You. ___

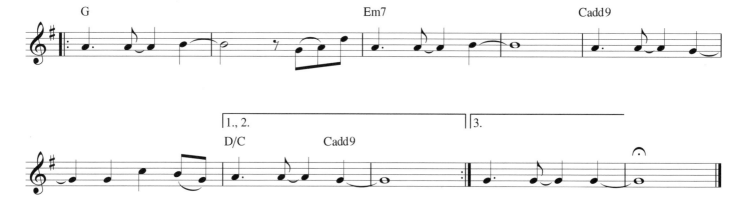

G   Em7   Cadd9

1., 2.   3.
D/C   Cadd9

Additional Lyrics

2. Oh, what I would do to have
The kind of strength it takes to stand before a giant
With just a sling and a stone,
Surrounded by the sound of a thousand warriors
Shaking in their armor,
Wishing they'd have had the strength to stand.
But the giant's calling out my name and he laughs at me,
Reminding me of all the times I've tried before and failed.
The giant keeps on telling me time and time again,
"Boy, you'll never win."
"You'll never win."

Wait for Me

Words and Music by Rebecca St. James

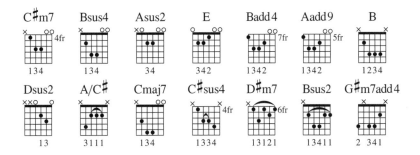

*Tune down 1/2 step:
  (low to high) E♭–A♭–D♭–G♭–B♭–E♭

Strum Pattern: 4
Pick Pattern: 2

Intro
Moderately

*Optional: To match recording, tune down 1/2 step.

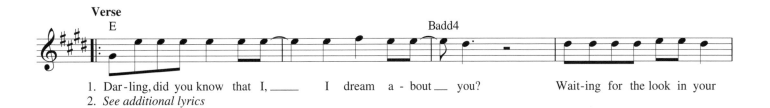

1. Dar-ling, did you know that I, ___ I dream a-bout ___ you? Wait-ing for the look in your
2. *See additional lyrics*

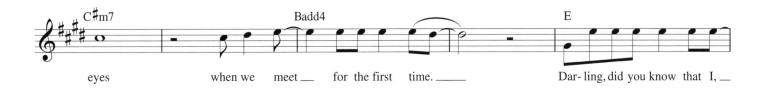

eyes when we meet ___ for the first time. ___ Dar-ling, did you know that I, ___

___ I pray a-bout ___ you? Pray-ing that you ___ will hold on. Keep your

lov-ing eyes on-ly for me. 'Cause I am wait-ing for, ___ pray-ing for ___ you, dar-

Badd4   C#m7   Asus2

ling. _____   Wait for me _____ too, _____   wait for me as ___ I wait _ for you.

Bsus4   E   Badd4

'Cause I am wait-ing for, _____ pray-ing for ___ you, dar - ling. _____

To Coda ⊕

             C#m7   Asus2

Wait for me _____ too, _____ wait for me as _____ I wait _ for you.

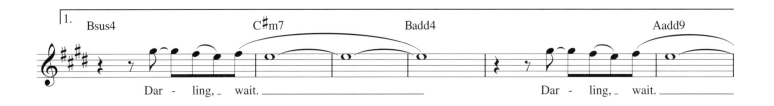

1. Bsus4   C#m7   Badd4   Aadd9

Dar - ling, _ wait. _____   Dar - ling, _ wait. _____

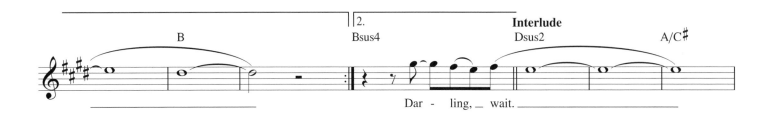

         B   2. Bsus4   **Interlude** Dsus2   A/C#

                 Dar - ling, _ wait. _____

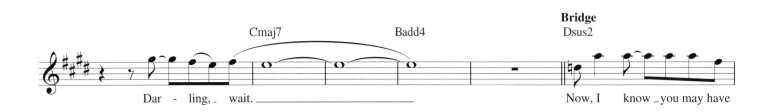

       Cmaj7   Badd4   **Bridge** Dsus2

Dar - ling, _ wait. _____   Now, I know _ you may have

       A/C#   Asus2

made mis-takes, _____   but there's for-give - ness _ and a sec-ond chance. _

So, wait for me, dar - ling, wait for me.

D.S. al Coda

Wait for me. Wait for me, for me. _____ 'Cause I am

⊕ Coda

Outro-Chorus

'Cause I am wait-ing for, _ pray-ing for _ you, dar - ling. _ Wait for me _____

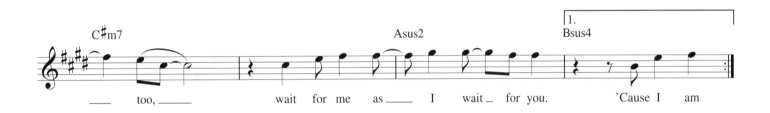

_____ too, _____ wait for me as _____ I wait _ for you. 'Cause I am

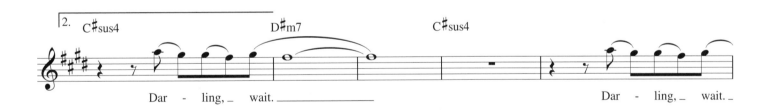

Dar - ling, _ wait. _____ Dar - ling, _ wait. _

Wait _ for _____ me.

Additional Lyrics

2. Darling, did you know I dream about life together,
Knowing it will be forever?
I'll be yours and you'll be mine.
And, darling, when I say, "Till death do us part,"
I'll mean it with all of my heart.
Now and always faithful to you.

We Are One Tonight

Words and Music by Jonathan Foreman and Tim Foreman

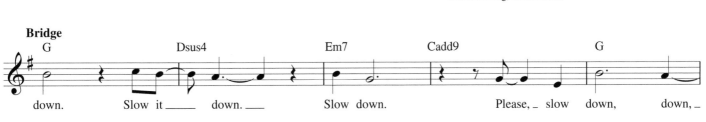

What If

Words and Music by Jadon Lavik, Adam Watts and Andy Dodd

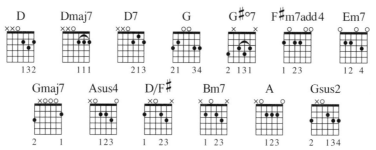

Strum Pattern: 2, 3
Pick Pattern: 4, 5

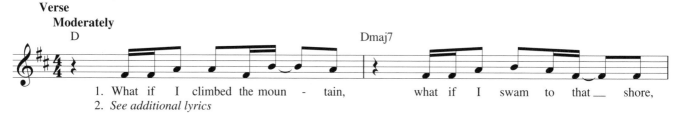

1. What if I climbed the moun - tain, what if I swam to that __ shore,
2. *See additional lyrics*

what if ev - 'ry bat - tle was __ vic - to - r'ous, then would You love me more, __

would You love me more? __

world that keeps chang-ing, there's one thing that I know ___ is true: Your love is stay-ing. There's

noth-ing else _ I hold on _____ to. ___ You say I be-long _ to

You a - part from the things _ I do. You say I be-long to

You. I'm in awe ___ of why You _ do, ___ why _ You do. _ ___ I'm in

awe _____ of ___ You, ___ I'm in awe _____ of _____ You. ___

Outro
w/ voc. ad lib. on repeats

Repeat and fade

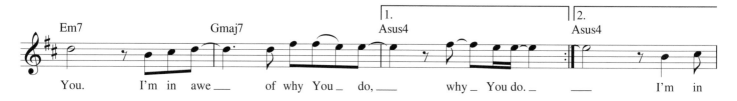

The way You love me, ___ the way You do. ___

Additional Lyrics

2. What if I ignored the hand that fed me,
What if I forgot to confess,
What if I stumbled down that mountain,
Then would You love me less? Lord, would You love me less?
What if I were ev'ryone's last choice,
What if I mixed in with the rest,
What if I failed what I passed before,
Then would You love me less? Lord, would You, would You love me less?
Oh, no, oh no, oh no.

When It's Time to Go

Words and Music by Jeff Silvey and Billy Simon

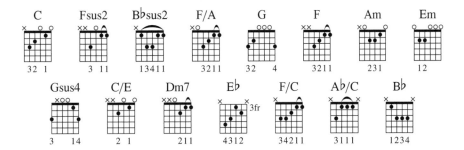

Strum Pattern: 2
Pick Pattern: 4

Verse
Moderately

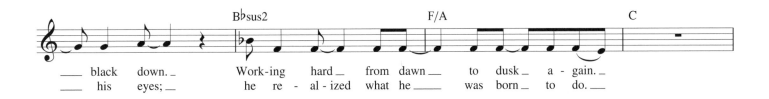

1. Noth-ing new __ in this __ old town, the sun comes up __ and heads __
2. Some years lat - er late __ one night __ he came in try'n' __ to dry __

__ black down. Work-ing hard __ from dawn __ to dusk __ a-gain. __
__ his eyes; __ he re - al - ized what he __ was born __ to do. __

Sev - en - teen __ and a heart __ for a change, the by-ways call - ing out __
He said I'll al - ways __ be your __ son __ and I know you __ know what's

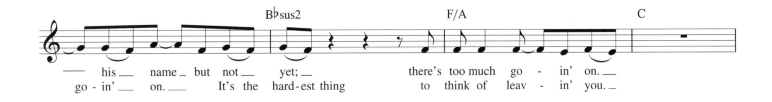

__ his __ name __ but not __ yet; __ there's too much go - in' on. __
go - in' __ on. __ It's the hard-est thing to think of leav - in' you. __

'Cause dad - dy needs __ a hand and ma - ma's ten - der heart __ might
But this world needs __ a hand and I've __ got just the thing __ they

crum - ble to ___ the ground. Though they'd un - der - stand, _ He felt like say- ing:
need to make _ it through. It's so clear to me ___ though I know what's com- ing.

Chorus

When it's time _ to go, ___ you've got ___ to let me go ___ a - way ___ and face _ the

world. (Say good - bye.) ___ Say good - bye. ___ Cry some tears, ___ don't wor - ry.

When I hit ___ the cit - y, I'll ___ build you a house _ right down the street _ from

mine. _ Have _ some faith ___ in me ___ and I'll show you why. _

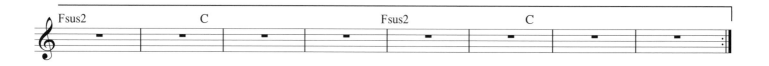

Bridge

And as they tore His flesh like an - i - mals, ___ there were those I

190

know   who   felt   Him   say: _____

Chorus
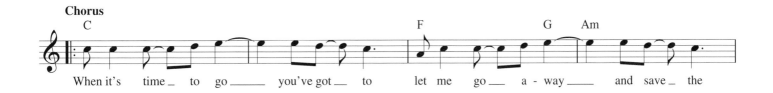
When it's   time _ to go _____ you've got _ to   let   me   go   a - way _____ and   save _ the

world. _ (Say good - bye.) _   Say good - bye. _   Cry some   tears, _ don't wor - ry.   When   I   hit _ the cit -

- y, I'll _ build   you   a   house _ right   down   the   street _ from   mine. _   Oh, _

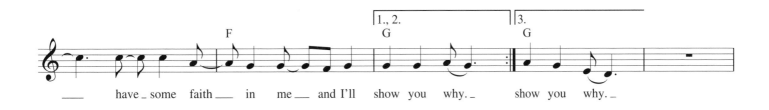
____   have _ some   faith _   in   me _   and I'll   show   you   why. _   show   you   why. _

When You Are a Soldier

Words and Music by Steven Curtis Chapman

Bridge

will be ___ the one you ___ can cry your song ___ to. My ___ eyes will share ___ your

tears. I'll ___ be your friend if ___ you win or if

you're de-feat-ed. When-ev-er ___ you need ___ me. I will ___ be here.

Outro

When you're lost ___ in dark-ness, I will hold ___ the light. ___ I will help ___ you

find your way ___ through the night. ___ I'll re-mind ___ you of the truth ___ and keep the flame ___

___ a-live in you. ___ And I will be ___ your shield, 'cause

I know how ___ it feels ___ when you are ___ a sol - dier. ___ And

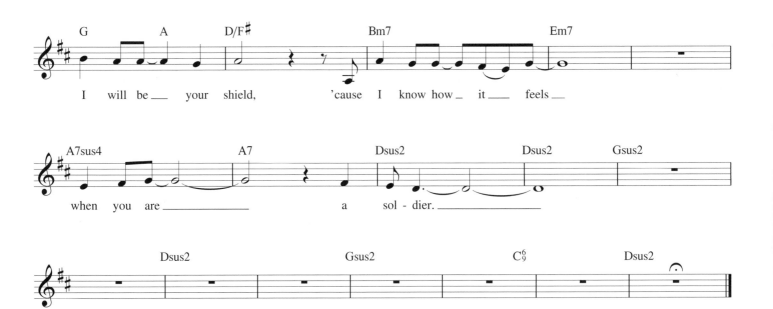

I will be __ your shield, 'cause I know how __ it __ feels __
when you are _____ a sol - dier. _____

Word of God Speak

Words and Music by Bart Millard and Pete Kipley

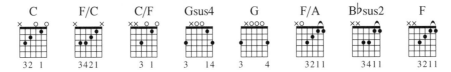

Strum Pattern: 4
Pick Pattern: 4

1. I'm find-ing my - self __ at a loss for words, and the fun-ny thing is, it's o-
   my - self __ in the midst of You, be-yond the mu - sic, __ be-yond the

kay. The last thing I need __ is to be heard, but to hear what You would
noise. All that I need __ is to be with You, and in the qui-et hear Your

Chorus

say. }
voice. }   Word of God, speak. __ Would You pour down like rain, __ wash-ing my eyes __

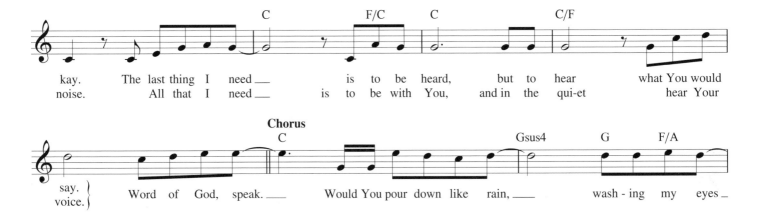

___ to see Your maj - es - ty? To be still and know __ that You're in this place._

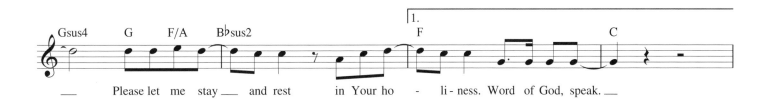

___ Please let me stay __ and rest in Your ho - li - ness. Word of God, speak. ___

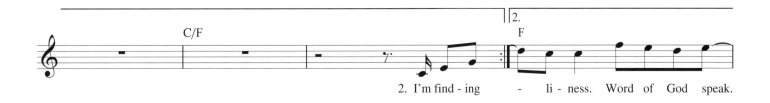

2. I'm find - ing - li - ness. Word of God speak.

___ Would You pour down like rain, __ wash - ing my eyes __ to see Your maj -_

_- es - ty? To be still and know __ that You're in this place. __ Please let me stay ___

___ and rest in Your ho - li - ness. _____ I'm find - ing my -_

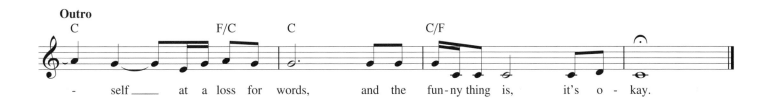

_- self __ at a loss for words, and the fun-ny thing is, it's o - kay._

195

Where There Is Faith

Words and Music by Billy Simon

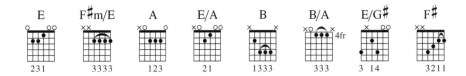

Strum Pattern: 2
Pick Pattern: 2

voice call - ing: "Keep walk - ing, you're not _ a - lone in _ this world."

Where there _ is faith there is _ a peace like _ a child sleep - ing,

hope ev - er - last - ing _ in He who _ is a - ble to bear ev - 'ry

bur - den, _ to heal ev - 'ry hurt in _ my heart. It is _ a

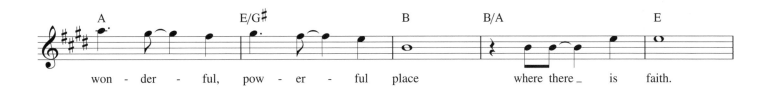

won - der - ful, pow - er - ful place where there _ is faith.

Additional Lyrics

2. There's a man across the sea,
Never heard the sound of freedom ring,
Only in his dreams.
There's a lady dressed in black,
In a motorcade of Cadillacs.
Daddy's not coming back.
Our hearts begin to fall and our stability grows weak,
But Jesus meets our needs
If only we believe.

Who Am I

Words and Music by Mark Hall

Wholly Yours

Words and Music by David Crowder

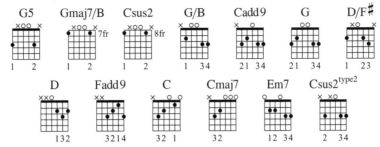

*Capo II

Strum Pattern: 2
Pick Pattern: 3

Verse
Moderately

1. I am full of __ earth, You are heav - en's _ worth. I am stained with __ dirt,

* Optional: To match recording, place capo at 2nd fret.

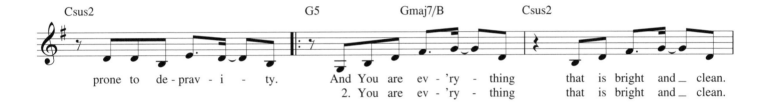

prone to de - prav - i - ty. And You are ev - 'ry - thing that is bright and __ clean.
2. You are ev - 'ry - thing that is bright and __ clean.

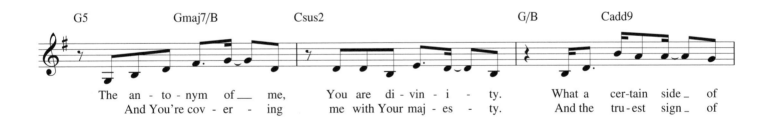

The an - to - nym of __ me, You are di - vin - i - ty. What a cer - tain side _ of
And You're cov - er - ing me with Your maj - es - ty. And the tru - est sign _ of

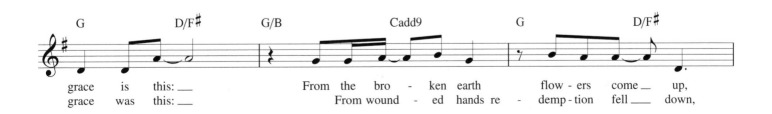

grace is this: __ From the bro - ken earth flow - ers come _ up,
grace was this: __ From wound - ed hands re - demp - tion fell __ down,

Chorus

push-ing through _the dirt.
lib - er - a - ting man.
And You are ho - ly, ho - ly ho - ly. All heav-en cries, "Ho -

- ly, ho - ly ___ God." ___ Oh, You are ho - ly, ho - ly, ho -

To Coda

1.

- ly. I want to be ho - ly like _ You _ are. ___

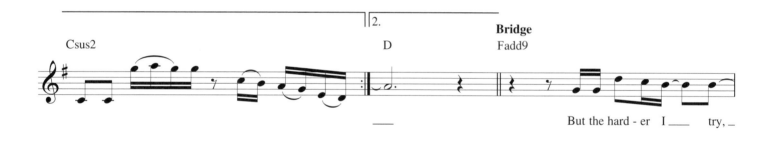

2.

Bridge

___ But the hard - er I ___ try, _

___ the more clear - ly can I ___ feel the depth _ of our fall ___ and the weight of it all.

And so this ___ might could be ___ the most im - pos - si - ble thing, _ Your grand-ness in me, _

mak - ing me clean. Glo - ry, hal - le - lu - jah! Glo - ry, glo - ry, hal -

D.S. al Coda

𝄌 **Coda**

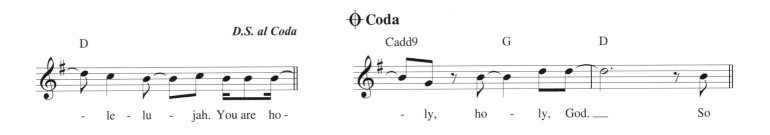

- le - lu - jah. You are ho - - ly, ho - ly, God. __ So

Pre-Chorus

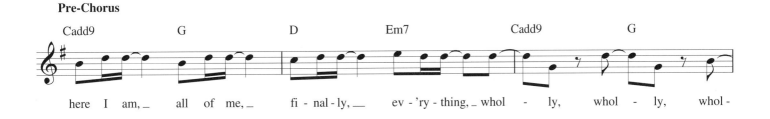

here I am, __ all of me, __ fi - nal - ly, __ ev - 'ry - thing, __ whol - ly, whol - ly, whol -

Chorus

_- ly. ____ I am whol - ly, whol - ly, whol - ly, I am whol - ly, whol - ly, whol-_

Outro

_- ly __ Yours._ I am whol - ly Yours. __

* Use Pattern 10

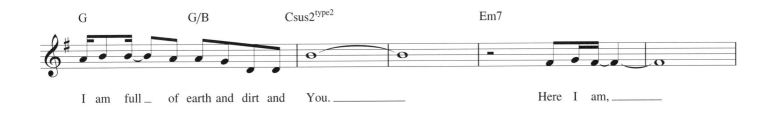

I am full __ of earth and dirt and You. _____ Here I am, _____

**Repeat and fade**

ev - 'ry - thing.

Wisdom

Words and Music by Twila Paris

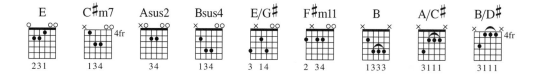

Strum Pattern: 1
Pick Pattern: 4, 5

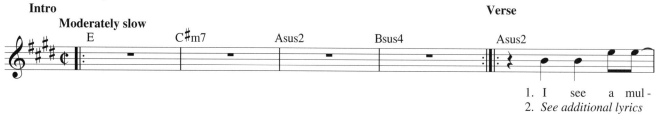

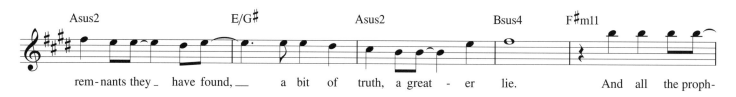

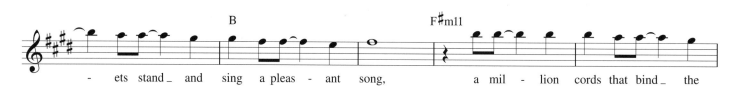

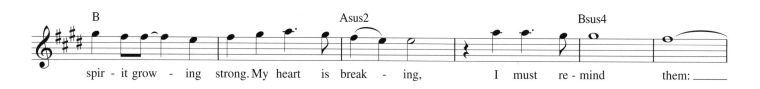

Additional Lyrics

2. There is a moment of decision,
But all the days go rushing by,
An undercurrent of confusion
To threaten all that we believe, with little time to wonder why.
And all the prophets sing the same familiar song.
Even the chosen can be led to sing along.
These hearts are breaking, will You remind us:

You

Words and Music by Josh Havens, Matt Fuqua, Brad Wigg and Marc Dodd

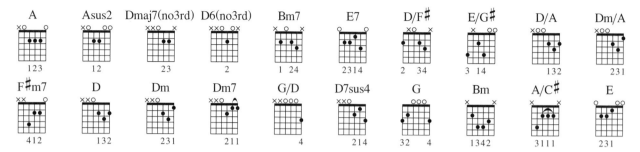

*Tune down 1/2 step:
(low to high) E♭–A♭–D♭–G♭–B♭–E♭

Strum Pattern: 2, 6
Pick Pattern: 5

Verse
Moderately

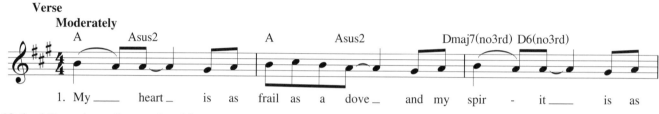

1. My ___ heart ___ is as frail as a dove ___ and my spir - it ___ is as

*Optional: To match recording, tune down 1/2 step.

weak as a rose. ___ See my sor - row, feel ___ my pain. ___ You're my ref -

- uge, ___ You're ___ my rea - son, ___ my ___ strength in ___ this beau - ti - ful place. ___

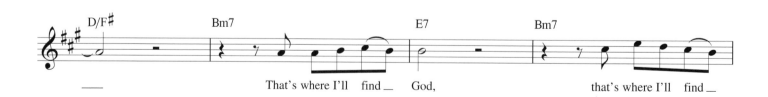

___ That's where I'll find ___ God, that's where I'll find ___

God, oh, ___ oh. ___ You're in my heart, ___ You're in my soul. ___ You are my heav-

- en, You're_ my __ home. __ You're my best friend, __ You're my true love. __

To Coda ⊕

Interlude

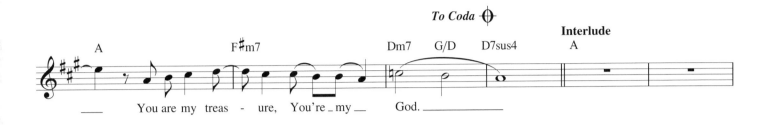

__ You are my treas - ure, You're_ my __ God. _____

Verse

2. I _____ watch _ as the moun-tains fall down __ and the

riv - ers ___ part at Your feet. __ Your cre - a - tion sings _ Your praise. _

__ E - ven winds _ o - bey _ and an - gels _ bow down at __ Your

beau - ti - ful voice. __ That's where I find_ God. You're in my heart, _

⊕ **Coda**

D.S. al Coda

Interlude

__ You're in my soul. _ ___ You're my __ God. _____

207

You're in my heart, __ You're in my soul. __ You are my heav-

-en, You're __ my __ home. __ You're my best friend, __ You're my true love. __

__ You are my treas - ure, You're __ my __ hope. __ You are my peace, __

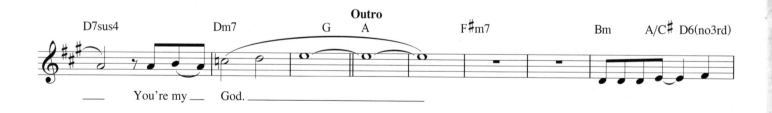

__ You are my joy. __ You are my Sav - ior, You're __ my __ God. __

__ You're my __ God. __